ESSENTIAL LIFE SKILLS FOR TEEN BOYS

EVERYTHING A TEEN NEEDS TO KNOW IN LIFE TO BE HAPPY. LIKE HOW TO BE AN A+ STUDENT, A CONFIDENT SPEAKER, HAVE ELECTRIC SOCIAL SKILLS, DATE, AND BE HEALTHY!

TEEN LIFE SKILLS

FREE GIFT

To thank you for reading our book, the Teen Life Skills team, who have achieved tremendous success in education, have decided to give our *"Teenage Guide To Academic Excellence"* away **FREE OF CHARGE**.

This guide has helped thousands of people improve their grades and build habits that will lead to consistent academic success.

To get your free copy, scan the QR Code on the next page and enjoy!

FREE GIFT

UNLOCKING ACADEMIC EXCELLENCE
WARNING
GENIUS AT WORK
The Ultimate Teen Guide to Achieving Better Grades
Teen Life Skills

ISBN: 978-1-915736-04-8 (Paperback)

ISBN: 978-1-915736-05-5 (Hardcover)

First printing edition 2023. Teen Life Skills

11816 Inwood Rd #

1291 Dallas, TX 75244

admin@teenlifeskill.com

REVIEW

Hey look a picture of me! Now that I have your attention please help this guy out.

If you want to spread some joy to my own life and the lives of our team at Teen Life Skills, please consider leaving a review of this book by scanning the QR Code below.

Your words can influence other parents' or teenagers' decisions to read this book. This helps us spread our message of self-improvement and allows the book to reach the hands of more people who need it.

Please consider leaving a review of this book; it takes 60 seconds and can make a real impact on our lives and the lives of our readers.

Thank you from the author of this book!

CONTENTS

INTRODUCTION

There once was a young boy named Robert. He roamed through his young life, constantly feeling like he could do more and become better. He couldn't shake the feeling that something was missing. He had good grades and a supportive family, but he couldn't help feeling like something was holding him back from reaching his full potential. This continued for most of his early teenage years until one day. Robert was in the library getting some books for an upcoming class assignment when he noticed an unusual book during his research, The 7 Habits of Highly Effective People by Stephen R. Covey. Immediately he was intrigued as he enjoyed reading, which was one of his favorite pastimes, but he mainly had read Harry Potter and other fiction books.

But this book seemed different, so he picked it up without overthinking it and rented it out along with the other books on his list. That weekend he decided to read a couple of pages, which turned out to him reading the entire book. This book introduced Robert to the idea that life was not predetermined but that our choices and the amount of effort we put in will decide our futures. Robert became obsessed with the idea of self-improvement and skill development. He decided to gather more books on similar topics.

He read different books, from goal setting to problem-solving to understanding the changes during puberty and how to navigate the transition to adulthood. He was particularly drawn to books on building confidence and emotional intelligence. He started putting the advice from these books into practice. He set a goal to make at least one new friend per month, and he was surprised at how easy it was once he started trying. He also began paying more attention to his hygiene and fashion. He was amazed at how much better he felt about himself. And soon, others noticed and complimented him more on his appearance. As his confidence grew, he started to think more seriously about what he wanted to do with his life. He had always been interested in business, so he set a goal to create his own company one day. He started researching different business ideas and networking with people in the industry.

As Robert approached graduation, he realized he had accomplished much more than he had ever thought possible. He had a group of close friends, a wonderful family, a loving girlfriend, and a clear plan for his future. He understood how fortunate he was to have found that first self-development book on that fateful day in the library and was now determined to put all his new lessons into practice. Years later, his business was thriving, and he was living his dream of being a successful entrepreneur. He always remembered the valuable lessons he learned from the books he had read and hoped to share all his knowledge with other teenagers also looking to improve themselves. And so, the story goes; Robert's life changed for the better, and he is now living a fulfilling life, all thanks to the knowledge he gained and put into practice.

Unfortunately, people usually only understand self-improvement and skill development when they are adults. By then, they have already wasted decades of potential growth. Our adolescence is the most important period of our lives. The skills you develop in understanding yourself and your objectives as a child and then a teen will serve you well throughout your life. Most people discover this truth too late to do anything about it.

Therefore, learning about yourself and your place in the world should begin as early as possible. You'll be much better off getting a head start on your learning. Taking your first step and getting this book is an excellent start to ensuring you have the life you have always dreamed of and grow up to be a man of high status, someone people respect, and, most importantly, a happy individual.

Now, if that young boy named Robert can pull it off, you can do it too with the help of *Essential Life Skills for Teen Boys*! This book is designed to guide you from a complete beginner in the world of self-improvement and skill development to being fully capable with the best chance to one day run your own business or get your dream job. Along the way, you'll learn the importance of family and friends and how to make and maintain those meaningful relationships. You'll find out how to optimize your brain power (the most important tool at our disposal) and learn essential secrets like dressing, acting, talking, and carrying yourself as a man of importance. Let's look at a fun fact: did you know the human brain doesn't stop developing until you're 25? That's right, your brain is still growing and changing, which means you have the potential to learn and achieve more than you ever thought possible.

That's great news for you because you have years to correct negative habits and develop ones that will put you lightyears ahead of any young teen who doesn't read this book. This means you'll have the best chance to be the captain of your sports team, be the best student in your class, be the most popular kid in your school, graduate with honors, go to your first-choice college, find love, marry the girl of your dreams, and succeed in every aspect of your life. So, grab a pen or pencil, make notes, and pay close attention to the secrets in this book because the teachings inside can change your life, just as they have changed so many others.

First, back to the earlier story, although I'm sure you could have guessed by now. I know the story of that young boy who began a life of self-improvement and now lives a life he could only have dreamed of because that young boy was me.

My name is Robert, and I am the owner and CEO of the company Teen Life Skills. Initially, I found remarkable success in business and finance in my late teens and early twenties. I decided to take what I have learned with all those years of entrepreneurship, public speaking, networking, attending college, building relationships, dating, and everything else I have learned thus far to help the next generation of aspiring teenagers. I know how hard it can be to find information tailored to teenagers. I had to read books far too advanced for my level when I began. And I can only wish I had a company such as Teen Life Skills that was available back when I started my journey—as I would be even further ahead of where I am now.

Our mission at Teen Life Skills is to help teenagers learn all the vital information they need to create a good life that makes them happy. It's as simple and straightforward as that; all our products are designed with that in mind. What makes this teenage life skill book so unique is the level of research that has been combined with personal life experience. I have already navigated most of the challenges you will face as a young man. Even if I didn't tackle the problems correctly then, I now have the added benefit of hindsight or the ability to reflect and see what I could have done better.

Before I entered the entrepreneurial world and started my business, I had a career as a scientist. You'll hear me occasionally discuss my days at college, where I studied Biological Chemistry. My time as a scientist in college and the pharmaceutical industry has allowed me to research, read, and break down scientific studies like few others. Why is this important for you? This is important because, throughout this book, you will see first-class scientific studies explained so that you can easily understand and implement the learnings in your own life.

So, where other books might be able to pull research from average, aged, or incorrect sources, you can rest assured that with this book and the others produced by my publishing company, you are getting the most up-to-date, scientifically proven, and accurate methods of improving your life skills. Of course, we won't address every possible concern you have.

Everyone leads a unique life, and your problems and issues will differ from other teens in your town, state, or country. If we were to address all the possible concerns that teen boys could face, we would have a book that is over 10,000 pages in length. With that in mind, we have chosen essential life skills that teen boys must learn. If you take the time to develop these skills, we guarantee you will lead a more fulfilling, successful, and happy life. So, whether you're just starting high school or getting ready to graduate, this book is here to help you make the most of your teenage years. You can accomplish anything with the right skills and a positive attitude.

So, are you ready to transform your life? Let's get started!

Before we move on to the first chapter, I should explain the nature of this book and the series to follow. As you have already noticed, this book is designed for teenage boys, and we have a second book in the series being produced for teenage girls. It is impossible to help teenagers develop life skills and lead happy lives without speaking specifically about the problems they might face. Teenagers, in general, will face several similar issues as they navigate into adolescence. But to ensure the absolute best outcome for every teen that reads our work, we have taken that extra step to ensure you have the best possible information tailored to your life to help you take on the world.

1

THE MOST IMPORTANT SKILL

Time appears to rush by at an alarming rate, and life never seems to slow down. One day you're relaxing in school with your friends. Then suddenly, you're an adult with your own family and responsibilities. When that moment arrives, we must be ready to confront the obstacles that life throws at us. And that is this book's sole purpose of preparing you for a successful life abundant with wealth, success, status, and most importantly, happiness. Not everyone will have the same visions of their dream life, and that's completely normal. Both you and your best friend could have completely different goals and plans for your life. That's why, within every chapter of this book, we have provided the absolute best information, skills, practices, and techniques to help you improve every aspect of your life, no matter your dreams.

So, pay close attention as you read this book, and don't hesitate to mark the pages and make notes to help absorb the information. In this chapter, we'll look at the power of the human mind and why developing excellent habits as a teenager can lead to incredible results for you as an adult.

The mind is your most powerful instrument. We will highlight some essential skills connected to the teenage mind. We will discuss the mentality and practices that will assist you in achieving your goals and living a successful life. We state that the mind and all associated skills are the most important skills for a teenage boy to develop because, without the proper mindset, you will not develop other skills successfully.

You need to create a mindset that will allow you to fail and not immediately achieve the desired results. There are very few worthwhile activities, skills, or experiences in life that you can try for the first time and be an expert. Life is all about trial and error, and the most successful people are the ones who are willing to fail, fail, and fail but never give up. You need to be content with the fact that simply reading this book won't be enough to master the life skills required to be a successful man. You will need to take the lessons in each chapter and apply them to your life, and to do that you need your most powerful tool, the mind!

POSITIVE THINKING

Positive thinking is not just one of those self-help mantras that people with long braided hair would preach at your local hippie commune. In all truth, positive thinking is one of the most potent tools that successful athletes, CEOs, entrepreneurs, singers, actors, and all the people who achieve great things in life use daily. Why would such powerful, successful, and influential people use positive thinking? Well, the truth is that there are only two ways you can look at the world. It could be through a negative lens (pessimistic view) or a positive lens (optimistic view). The way you decide to view the world can have a dramatic impact on your life and not just on your mood. Most people who achieve great things all point to a "never say die" attitude or simply "never take no for an answer." They constantly try to look at their current situation in the most upbeat and positive way possible.

Imagine you were one of the world's foremost entrepreneurs, and your business has been booming for years. However, one day you wake up to find that your business has begun to fail. Slowly, day by day, you watch the business you have spent your life building melt away until, eventually, your company is bankrupt, and you have lost millions. So, what are your options now? There are only two things you can do; give up and do nothing and accept your new life or say to yourself, "I've built an empire once; I can do it again." What attitude do you think has a better chance of bringing you to your desired outcome? And sure, there is no guarantee that the next business you try will be successful. Still, if you honestly never give up, you cannot fail, and eventually, things will once again turn in your favor.

People who engage in positive thinking tend to have better psychological and physical health, are more resilient in the face of adversity, and experience greater success in their personal and professional lives. Positive thinking is a powerful tool to create a happier and more fulfilling life. It's like a muscle. The more you use it, the stronger it gets; it can change how you think and feel (Positive Thinking: Stop Negative Self-talk to Reduce Stress, 2022).

The Health Benefits of Positive Thinking

Besides the fantastic benefits of positive thinking in your career, business, school/college, or social life, it also has several tremendous health benefits. Let's take a quick look at some of the notable benefits below:

- It can help you feel less stressed and anxious.
- It can help you sleep better at night.
- It can boost your immune system and make you less likely to get sick.
- It can lower your blood pressure and reduce your risk of heart disease.
- It can help you feel more energized and improve your overall mood.
- It can make you feel happier and more satisfied with your life.

Lisa R. Yanek of Johns Hopkins University School of Medicine published an article in The American Journal of Cardiology in 2013. The study was conducted on people with a family history of coronary artery disease. Those who adopted positive thinking were 13% less likely to have a heart attack than those who didn't adopt positive thinking (Yanek, 2013). This study showed a link between a positive outlook and a prolonged and healthier life. Isn't that amazing? Simply by looking at the bright side of life, you can reduce your chance of illness. Wouldn't you agree that it is at least worth a try?

Optimistic and cheerful people are also believed to live better lives. They have a better physique, find it easier to make new friends, and typically make more money. Have you ever met someone with such a contagious smile and upbeat attitude that it would genuinely bring happiness to your life by simply being with them? The opposite is also true. No one likes to spend time with someone negative as it draws the energy out of the room. So, if you're trying to impress in work, school, college, or simply make new friends, consider the type of person you would like to hang out with and act similarly. By now, you are eager to begin implementing more positive thinking in your own life after reading about the fantastic results. So, let's look at a method of positive thinking and outline how it can improve our lives and health.

THE PLACEBO EFFECT

One such method of positive thinking is known as the placebo effect. You might have already heard of this phenomenon, as it is present in almost every pharmaceutical study of a new drug approved by the FDA. All new medicines a pharmaceutical company wants to bring to market must prove to the regulatory body that they can show better results than a placebo drug.

But what is a placebo drug? A placebo drug is a fake treatment given to a control group of participants during a scientific study for a potential drug.

One group of patients is given the real drug, and one group is given the fake drug (placebo drug). Usually, both groups believe they are receiving the real drug. This is so the scientists can measure the difference in safety & efficacy (ability to achieve the desired result) between the real drug and the placebo to determine whether the real drug is more effective than the placebo or not. It turns out that when people take a prescribed drug and simply believe it will positively impact their situation, the phycological phenomenon of the placebo can actually have a positive effect just due to someone's expectations.

In 2014, a study was published by Slavenka Kam-Hansen of Beth Israel Deaconess Medical Center, Harvard Medical School, Boston. This study explains how the placebo effect goes beyond believing that therapy or an operation will work. It is about strengthening the relationship between our brain and body (Kam-Hansen et al., 2014). The study showed that our brains can influence our bodies and improve specific symptoms of the problem our body is experiencing. This means placebos can make you feel better but can't fix things like high cholesterol, diabetes, heart disease, or tumors. They help with things your brain controls, like feeling less pain, being unable to sleep because of stress, and feeling sick from cancer treatment.

According to the study mentioned earlier, placebos aren't just fake pills. You can also give yourself a placebo by doing healthy things. This includes eating well, exercising, practicing yoga, hanging out with friends, and meditating. All these things can make you feel better in the same way that taking a fake pill can. The body's response to a placebo can be explained by the release of endorphins and other chemicals in the brain. Endorphins are natural painkillers released in response to certain stimuli, like exercise. Placebos can also affect the release of other chemicals in the brain, like dopamine and serotonin, influencing your mood and overall well-being. So how can you use the placebo effect to improve your own life?

Although the placebo works best when people don't know they are taking a false medication, it is still effective even when they know it is a placebo. This means just the simple act of taking something people believe to be helpful to their situation can help their life.

This means we can use the placebo effect to improve our health, even if we know it's a placebo. Look at the list below and try to implement these placebos into your own life each week:

1. Take a multivitamin and genuinely believe this will boost your immune system. This will lower cortisol (the stress hormone) and boost your immune system.
2. No matter how well you slept the night before, wake up and say wow, I feel refreshed today. This will improve your focus and attention for the day ahead.
3. Drink a cup of coffee before you study or work out and believe in the performance-enhancing effects of caffeine.
4. Take a cold shower and say to yourself, "wow, I feel so refreshed, focused, and my mood is so much better after the shower."
5. Drink plenty of water throughout the day, and after each sip, glass, or bottle, think to yourself how this water is helping your system perform at its best.

Each of the above is just an example; you can really use any positive stimulus (something that causes a change) in your life as the starting point to use the placebo effect. It could be opening a book to study, sitting attentively in class, saying hello and goodnight to loved ones, eating healthy, exercising, maintaining good hygiene, or anything positive you want to reinforce. Each time you perform the stimulus, try to imagine all the wonderful things the act is giving your life. And after enough time, this will lead to a more positive mindset and more of the actual result you were trying to achieve from the stimulus using the placebo effect.

The placebo effect works for the examples above because each method improves the chance of the desired outcome. For example, multivitamins boost your immune system, sleep enhances focus, and coffee is a performance enhancer for study and exercise. But the placebo effect is not a miracle worker; you can't take a multivitamin and suddenly grow a foot taller. Or take a jog and start believing your Usain Bolt. Or drink some coffee and pass a test you didn't study for.

It can benefit your life in many ways. However, a placebo effect focuses mainly on the mind and body connection, so it works best for stress, sleep, mood, and mental performance.

How to Use Positive Thinking to Make Your Life Better

let's say you're about to talk to a new group of friends. If you're thinking positive thoughts, you might tell yourself, "I'm going to make some great friends today" or "I'm a great conversationalist; I got this!" This positive thinking can boost confidence and make it easier for you to start a conversation. Or you have a test or exam coming up. Instead of thinking, "I'm going to fail, I'm not good at this," try to think positive thoughts like "I've studied hard, I'm prepared, and I'm going to do great" or "I'm capable of doing well, and I'll give it my best shot." This positive thinking can help you feel less anxious and more confident about the exam.

Similarly, positive thinking can improve your feelings about a presentation or job interview. Instead of thinking, "I'm going to mess up," tell yourself, "I've practiced, I'm ready, and I'm going to do a great job," or "I'm excited to show what I know." This positive thinking can increase your confidence and help you feel more prepared and ready for the task. Remember, it's not always easy to be positive, but with practice, you can learn to think more positively and improve your life.

Positive Thinking Exercises

Besides the placebo effect, you can use some of the other exercises below to improve your positive thinking skills.

Gratitude journal: A gratitude journal is a simple yet powerful way to develop a positive mindset. This exercise involves writing down three things you're grateful for each day. It can be anything—big or small—from the people in your life, the food you ate, or the nice weather. Focusing on the positive things in your life will train your brain to look for the good in every situation. This exercise can be done at the end of the day or in the morning to start your day positively.

Positive visualization: Positive visualization is a powerful way to change your mindset and achieve your goals. The exercise involves a few minutes to close your eyes and imagine yourself performing a specific goal or outcome. It could be anything from getting a good grade on an upcoming test, making a new friend, or scoring the winning goal for a sports game. As you imagine yourself achieving the goal, add as much detail as possible. See yourself in the situation, feel the emotions and sensations, hear the sounds and voices, and visualize how you would react. The idea is to make the visualization as vivid and authentic as possible. This exercise can help rewire your brain to believe the goal is achievable and increase your motivation and confidence.

Positive thinking is a terrific way to make your life better. It can help you feel more confident and excited about things. It can help you focus on the good and see the best in every situation. Positive thinking can help you to do well in school, make friends, and even make you happier. So, start thinking positively today! The following section will discuss another powerful way to improve your life: developing a growth mindset.

Growth Mindset

According to Professor Carol Dweck, an American Psychologist who coined the term growth mindset, it is the concept that you can improve your talents and abilities by putting in the effort, using the proper tactics, and seeking advice from others (What Having a "Growth Mindset" Actually Means, 2022). A person with a growth mindset believes they can improve on anything if they keep the right attitude and put in consistent hard work. It's the opposite of thinking you're not good at something and can't change. For example, a person with a growth mindset can improve on a bad math grade by saying, "I know I performed poorly on this test. But if I put in more work, trust my ability, and get the proper assistance, I can get a much better grade next time." A person with a fixed mindset would say, "Look, another bad grade. I'm just terrible with math." Both people received the same grade.

The only difference was one person had a growth mindset, and the other had a fixed mindset. This will lead the person with the growth mindset to improve in the future because they will put in more work, and the other person will either stay the same or worsen as they lose more confidence.

How Effective Is The Growth Mindset?

A growth mindset appeared in research published in the International Journal of STEM Education in 2020 by Lisa B. Limeri from the Department of Biochemistry & Molecular Biology, University of Georgia. It turns out that doing well in school can change how students think about school (Limeri, 2020). This means that if the person begins on the right foot and is doing well, their confidence will be higher, and they will believe they can get good grades again. This positive feedback loop will help them achieve more good grades because they are likelier to pay attention in class and study harder.

My greatest transformation during my teenage years was discovering and developing a growth mindset. If done successfully, there is nothing you can't do. Of course, you might not be able to join a team in the NBA, but if you love basketball and practice every day with the belief that you will get better, I can guarantee you will reach your full potential. Just think about the power of this slight mindset shift; suddenly, our weaknesses become opportunities to develop more as a person.

I was once a shy kid who could never get my words out. If I were asked to perform in a school play, read aloud, or give an answer in class, I would avoid the opportunity, and if I had to, I would quietly struggle my way through it. I knew I had to improve on this skill, and once I discovered that I could improve, this was the fuel I needed to practice. Firstly it was at home reading to myself aloud in my room; then it was acting the speech out in my mirror, then it was in the classroom, and today? I regularly give speeches to large audiences with confidence and a powerful voice.

This is one of many examples of where I went from a complete beginner in a skill and slowly clawed my way to reaching my full potential with the help of a growth mindset. Trust yourself and stop saying things like, "I am bad at math, I can't do that, I'll never reach this goal, I am a failure." If you say something often enough, you will begin to believe it, so stop giving fuel to your weaknesses and flip the script. Begin saying, "I will be good at math one day, I can do this, I will reach my goal, I will be successful." Don't underestimate the power of our thoughts and words.

Finally, as powerful as the growth mindset is, you must realize that without work, energy, or effort, things can't change. The right attitude is one step in improving, and another is putting the time into a skill, task, job, or goal. If you want to be the best version of yourself, you must dedicate the time and effort; simply saying you will reach the goal won't be enough.

MEMORY SKILLS

Want to ace your exams and impress your teachers with your incredible memory? Or are you tired of constantly forgetting your locker combination? Whatever your reason may be, we've got you covered. So, grab a notebook and get ready to unleash the full potential of your teenage brain! With a few fun and easy techniques, you can boost your memory power and advance your brain to the next level.

What Are Memory Skills?

Memory skills are special tricks or tools that help you remember things. For example, suppose you want to remember a list of items. In that case, you can use a memory technique called 'chunking' to group the items to make them easier to remember. You can learn different memory skills to help you remember things more efficiently.

Good memory is like a superpower. An excellent memory can help you develop a better social and professional network. You'd be surprised, but even a small thing like remembering someone's name the next time you see them makes you so much more likable in their eyes. Also, a top-tier memory can help you remember and prioritize important tasks and information to help you get ahead in school and work. It can also help you remember important dates like your family's birthdays so you can make them feel special and keep your relationships strong. Or imagine remembering the 23rd president of the United States, who won the 1998 FIFA world cup, or the answer to Mr. Ken's biology question, just like a supercomputer. That's what good memory skills can do for you!

How Memory Works

Scientists don't completely understand how memory works. It's like a mystery. But they know there are two types: short-term and long-term memory (Proven Techniques That Really Work to Improve Your Memory, 2022). Short-term memory is your memory for today. It's where you keep information while using it until you either discard it or move it to your long-term memory. Long-term memory is like a storage place for your brain. It keeps information from the past, sometimes from many years ago, but also from more recent events. It's like a memory bank where your brain saves things it wants to remember.

How to Develop Memory Skills

Let's look at some of the best scientifically proven techniques to help improve memory.

Association: One of the most effective ways to develop your memory skills is by using association.

This technique involves linking new information to something you already know. For example, if you're trying to remember a new word, try associating it with a picture or a similar word in your language. This will help you to remember the new word more easily. You can also associate the new information with a specific place or person. This will help you to remember where or when you learned the new information. For example, you meet a new guy called John, and you happen to meet John in Denver, so he now becomes John Denver. This way, you associate John's name with the place where you met him and where he lives. This can help you remember his name if you meet him again, and you also have some conversation starters as you remember where you met him.

Repetition: Repetition is another powerful memory technique. This technique involves repeating new information multiple times until it becomes firmly ingrained in your memory. You can repeat new information out loud or in your head, write it down, or use flashcards. This can help memorize study material, a new phone number, or a password.

Chunking: Chunking is a memory technique that involves breaking down large amounts of information into smaller, more manageable chunks. This makes it easier to remember and recall the information. For example, if you're trying to remember a long string of numbers, like a credit card number, try breaking it down into smaller groups of numbers, like the first four digits, the next four digits, and so on. Additionally, you can use mnemonics, short phrases, or sentences that help you remember a list of items, a name, or a fact.

Organizing information: Another way to develop your memory skills is by organizing the information you want to remember. In 2012, an article was posted on Taylor & Francis Online by Jeremy R. Manning and Michael J. Kahana from Princeton Neuroscience Institute and the University of Pennsylvania. This study showed that it's easier to remember things that are grouped (Manning & Kahana, 2012).

This can be done by creating a system to store and retrieve information, like creating a visual map, a calendar, or a to-do list.

For example, if you're trying to remember a list of items, try organizing them into categories, like groceries, school supplies, or clothes. Or, if you're trying to remember a schedule or a timeline, try creating a visual representation like a chart or a flowchart. This can help you to see the connections between different pieces of information, making it easier to remember and recall.

Good memory skills can help you as you go through life. It can make school easier by helping you remember things you learn in class. It can also help you in your future jobs by remembering important tasks and deadlines. And it can make personal relationships better by remembering special dates and events. So, strong memory skills can be useful in many areas. Here is an example of where a strong memory can make your life one hundred times easier:

Public speaking: Public speaking can be a great way to use your excellent memory. This can involve setting a goal to remember the main points of your speech and practicing speaking confidently in front of an audience. By practicing good memory skills and having a good memory, you can retain important information and speak confidently. This can help you develop leadership skills and be prepared for job interviews, presentations, and other professional opportunities. In my own personal life, I have had to draw upon my memory during countless public speaking events. During such an event, I try not to read off any cards or from a script to make myself appear more confident, credible, and professional. The crowds appreciate this and feel I have given them the respect of preparing for the presentation. Now, as confident as I might seem to the audience, of course, I am nervous on the inside. Nobody wants to be in front of a crowd and forget their next talking point.

Thankfully, I have used some of the memory exercises above, and they have helped me to memorize my speeches in a short amount of time. Being sure I know the information before the speech has given me the confidence to speak clearly and coherently to large audiences and deliver the points I wish to speak on.

CREATIVE THINKING

Do you ever feel stuck, and your life and thoughts seem to stagnate? Things might even be going well in your life, but you just don't see yourself making any more improvements and can't seem to think outside the box. Well, don't worry—the solution lies in this next section! Now we're going to dive into the world of creative thinking. This important mental skill can help you break free from the shackles of a poor imagination and improve your life. Creative thinking is the key to unlocking your full potential. Whether you want to develop new ideas, solve problems more effectively, or live a more fulfilling life, this skill will surely help.

What Is Creative Thinking?

Being creative means being brave and unafraid to try new things. After you have a bunch of ideas, you can try them out and see which works best. You look at things differently and consider how your ideas fit your goals. This is important at work because people who are good at being creative can develop new and better ways to do things. Here are some practical examples of how improving your creativity can help you deal with all of life's challenges:

Starting a business: Creative thinking can be used to develop new and innovative business ideas. You can use your creativity to identify a problem or need in your community and then come up with a solution to fill that need. For example, you could start a lawn care business, a tutoring service, or a dog-walking business. By starting your own business, you can learn valuable life skills like budgeting, marketing, and problem-solving, which can help you become more successful in the future.

Suppose entrepreneurship or owning your own business is something you would like to do when you're older. In that case, beginning at a young age is a great idea. Most of today's successful businesspeople started small businesses when they were younger. Some started huge tech companies, clothing lines, or even just selling some lemonade in their neighborhood; they all started somewhere.

Problem-solving: Creative thinking is an essential skill for problem-solving. You can use your creativity to develop new and innovative solutions to problems you encounter in school, work, or your personal life. For example, you can use your creativity to find new ways to study more effectively, improve your time-management skills, or deal with stress and anxiety. When I was sixteen, I was in my school's drama club, and we were performing a play. During rehearsals, one of the actors got sick and couldn't perform on the night of the show. We were all panicking, but I had an idea. I suggested we change the script and make the character a narrator instead of an actor. That way, the sick actor could still be a part of the play, and we could still perform. My idea was a hit, and the play turned out great! It shows that sometimes being creative means thinking on your feet and solving unexpected problems.

Reducing stress: Creative thinking can also be used to relax and reduce stress after a tough day. You can use your creativity to find new and interesting ways to unwind and de-stress, like writing, drawing, painting, or playing music. You can also use creative visualization to imagine a peaceful and calming scene, which can help you to relax, unwind, and reduce stress.

There are so many great projects you can use your creative skills on; let's look at some examples:

1. **Writing**: Writing can be a great way to express yourself and explore creativity. Whether writing short stories, poetry, or journaling, you can explore your thoughts, feelings, and emotions. It's a great way to reflect on the world around you and develop your writing skills. Writing can also be a great creative outlet for struggling with stress, anxiety, or other emotional issues. It can also help you to become more expressive and communicative.
2. **Art**: Art is another excellent way to use creativity and imagination to create something beautiful or meaningful. It is a resourceful way to channel your emotions and communicate your thoughts and feelings. Art allows you to explore different mediums and techniques to create something unique and personal, from drawing and painting to sculpturing, carving, and photography.
3. **Acting**: Acting is an effective way to use your creativity and imagination to bring characters to life. Whether in school plays, community theatre, or improvisation groups, acting allows you to explore different characters and emotions and develop your communication and public speaking skills. It can also be a supportive way to make new friends and have fun. Moreover, acting can be a great way to build self-

confidence and step out of your comfort zone. You might be on your way to becoming the next Brad Pitt or Denzel Washington.

These creative outlets—writing, art, and acting—offer various ways to channel your creativity and imagination and improve your life. Each provides a unique form of self-expression, stress relief, and skill development. They can also serve as a stepping stone for you to pursue a career in your areas of interest in the future. In today's modern electronic world, people make impressive sums of money internationally on writing platforms. This is where people bring their writing skills and sell them to others looking for blog writers, article writers, essay writers, CV writers, and many other forms of content creation. Perhaps you would like to start your writing career on one of these platforms and make some extra cash each week.

I'm sure you are familiar with the recent trend of NFTs and other artistic projects. People are becoming millionaires overnight by selling digital art. Of course, we won't make that kind of money (at least not right away). But if you're passionate about art and this is something you love, making it your full-time job is easier today than ever before. These are just a few examples of the many outlets and projects that can help you use your creative skills. The key is to find something that interests you and gives you the freedom and support to explore and develop your creativity.

IMPROVING FOCUS

So far in this chapter, we have discussed some vital mental skills we can develop in our teenage years to guarantee a successful life. And next up on that list of skills to master in your teenage years is focus.

Focus

Have you ever read something that doesn't make sense despite reading it over and over? Or have you been in class with your mind somewhere else, and you don't hear what the teacher is saying? Or have you been in a meeting thinking about something else and missed what was being discussed? When these things happen, it means you are not focusing.

According to Sabrina Romanoff, a Harvard-trained psychologist at Yeshiva University, you are said to be focused when you're really into something and not getting distracted. It's like when you're playing a video game and are so involved that you don't hear people talking to you or when you're reading a book and are not listening to people talking around you (What Is Focus? 2022). Being intelligent and doing well in school or work is hard to achieve without focus. When you can't focus, thinking clearly and understanding things is next to impossible. It's like trying to play a game while someone is constantly talking to you or trying to grab your attention. You can get things done faster and more efficiently when you're focused. When you're not focused, you can't work as well as you could. You might make mistakes or take longer to finish tasks.

Can You Improve Focus?

Research published in the International Journal of Environmental Research and Public Health in 2020 by Yi-Jung Lai from Wu Feng University and Kang-Ming Chang from Asia University examined how well kids can focus and pay attention in school. The researchers wanted to see if they could improve kids' focus by doing twelve-week special training. They picked 82 kids from the 5th and 6th grades to participate in the study. Half of the kids did the special training, and the other half didn't.

They gave all the kids a test to see how well they could focus and pay attention before and after the training. They determined that the kids who did the special training got better at focusing and paying attention than those who didn't. They also found that the kids who did the training said they could concentrate better in school and had an easier time falling asleep. Doing this special training can help kids do better in school by making them better at focusing and paying attention (Y. J. Lai & Chang, 2020).

Let's look at the method those scientists used in the study, which is also used by countless other professionals to improve focus.

Attention Training Therapy (ATT)

Professor Adrian Wells from the University of Manchester discovered this exercise, and there is a video you can watch on YouTube that has all three parts in one exercise. The video is 12 minutes long, with 5 minutes for the first part, 5 minutes for the second part, and 2 minutes for the third part.

Let's try this exercise. Follow the steps outlined below:

1. You can find this video on YouTube. Once you have the video, find a quiet place to sit or lie comfortably and with minimal distractions. Put on your headphones and press play.
2. You will listen to one sound at a time for the first part of the exercise. During this time, try to focus only on the sound you hear and nothing else. If your mind starts wandering, gently bring it back to the sound.
3. After the first section, the second part of the exercise will begin. During this time, you will be switching between different sounds. Try to focus on one sound, switch to another, and so on. This part is designed to help your mind be more flexible.
4. The final part of the exercise is designed to help you control negative thoughts and worries. During this time, you will listen to more than one sound simultaneously.

After the exercise, take some time to notice how you feel. You may feel more relaxed, focused, or less anxious. Remember that you can repeat this exercise as often as you want. The more you do it, the more your focus improves.

Brain Function and Focus

Different chemicals like epinephrine, acetylcholine, and dopamine control focus in our brains and body. Epinephrine, also known as adrenaline, is a chemical released in the brain and body and helps increase energy and alertness. However, it does not help with focus on its own. Acetylcholine is another chemical released in the brain; it works as a neurotransmitter (chemical neurons use to communicate) or neuromodulator (a messenger for signals between neurons). Acetylcholine plays a critical role in things like memory, learning, and focus. Increasing acetylcholine levels will increase brain plasticity and help you learn, focus and remember things better. The same is true for the opposite; if you have low levels of acetylcholine, the mental tasks mentioned above will be more difficult.

Ways You Can Optimize Acetylcholine Levels

Firstly, I will be reluctant to suggest you supplement to increase your acetylcholine levels even though it is one of, if not the best, ways to increase the levels in the body. Constant purchase and use of supplements can be expensive. I want to provide this teenage audience with the most useful and fitting information at no additional cost. Of course, suppose you are seriously deficient in any of the precursors or vitamins needed to produce acetylcholine. In that case, your body will likely need supplementation to maintain a healthy level. However, unless your doctor has instructed you to supplement for this deficiency, you should know that you can still optimize your levels by following the methods I list below. But of course, if you would like to take it to another level and use supplements, then by all means, do as it is another effective way of improving acetylcholine levels in the body. However, we won't be discussing any supplements in this book.

1. Optimizing zinc levels: Zinc plays a very important role in maintaining proper levels of acetylcholine. Zinc inhibits the enzyme acetylcholinesterase, and this enzyme breaks down acetylcholine. Since almost 2 billion people worldwide are deficient in zinc (Prasad, A. S. (2012), you can see why proper mineral levels are crucial to mental performance. Eat grass-fed beef, spinach, cashew nuts, mushrooms, or pumpkin seeds to increase your zinc levels.
2. Optimizing magnesium levels: Again, too many people have deficient levels of magnesium in their bodies. This mineral has an acceleration role in acetylcholine synthesis (production). Enjoys things like dark chocolate, avocados,

almonds, and bananas to have more magnesium levels in your body.

3. Eggs: An important precursor to acetylcholine production is choline, and eggs are among the richest sources of choline in our diets. If you can, and you enjoy them, try to eat more eggs during the week as they are great for focus levels and a great source of protein, and contain lots of healthy vitamins (Fallis, J. (2023, February 25)).

To improve focus, we can practice activities that help to increase the release of acetylcholine and dopamine in the brain, like attention training techniques. Additionally, getting enough sleep and maintaining a healthy lifestyle can help improve focus and attention.

Focus is an essential aspect of our daily lives. It helps us to achieve our goals and be successful in our pursuits. With the proper techniques and practices, you can improve your focus and attention and lead a more productive and successful life. In the next section, we will introduce you to the idea that we all have a set of principles or rules that guide us through life without us even knowing it. And if we can identify these rules, we will unlock the secret roadmap to living a fulfilling life.

2

FROM ADOLESCENCE TO ADULTHOOD

I remember constantly feeling lost and unsure of myself. I didn't know what to do with my life or what kind of person I wanted to be. My life lacked direction, and I wasn't sure how to approach any challenges or obstacles life threw at me. One day while reading through an article on the concept of meaning, I discovered a term I wasn't sure I had seen before. I certainly didn't understand what the author was referring to. So I began to research the topic. The term I am referring to is called "values." At first, I thought the author was simply speaking of the value of something or its price. But I soon realized through further reading exactly what values truly mean.

Everything changed once I discovered the power of understanding my values. It was like I had just uncovered the map to navigate my life in a manner that would keep me honest, balanced, and, most importantly, happy. I started asking myself questions like, what is important to me? What kind of person do I want to be? What are my priorities in life? And then, I discovered that my values are integrity, compassion, honesty, respect, hard work, and faith. Understanding my values helped me make better decisions and become more successful.

Are you tired of feeling lost and unsure of who you are and what you want? We have something that might change that. This chapter will help you figure out what's truly important to you and how to become the person you want to be. It will help you discover your values, make better decisions, and lead a more fulfilling life. In the same way that it's okay to be different from the values discussed in this book, it's also okay to disagree with them. You don't need to agree with the values I listed as my personal values or even agree with the traditional values of being a man. You'll be able to develop your own values with the help of the teachings outlined in this chapter. Values are like a guide that helps us make important decisions. They help us figure out what kind of person we want to be and how we want to treat ourselves and others. They also help us decide how we want to act in the world around us. Think of them like a set of rules you can use to make choices (What Are Values? 2018).

6 VALUES THAT ARE TYPICAL OF A MAN

I have already listed some of the values that are important to me. But if we were to look at a typical or traditional man, what values would you expect them to hold?

1. Compassion

Compassion means caring about and trying to help others who are in need. Once, during my college years, I sat in my lecture hall after class, finishing some notes before heading home for the day. I noticed another guy sitting in the back of the class too. This wasn't unusual as people often stayed after class to finish some work. But I noticed that this guy didn't appear to be taking notes or doing any work; he seemed quite upset. I could have left the class that day without giving it a second thought, but I decided to go up the steps and ask him if everything was okay. At first, he was a little tentative, so I decided to ask his name and begin a more general conversation about college and life. Eventually, he began to open up. He was from a different country where English was not his first language.

He was beginning to struggle with the fast-paced nature of college, and since every lesson was tough in English, it was extra tough for him. I sat and listened to his story for a few minutes and began feeling an uneasiness in my body. I began feeling empathic toward this guy and decided I needed to do something. I decided to give him my number and said if ever he needed anything to give me a call, whether it was about college or even just for a chat. We began meeting once a week to discuss our course and put our heads together to see what we could learn. Initially, I was doing a lot of the teaching, but soon I was getting more insight and help from him than the other way around. Eventually, he began to feel more confident in class and in general, and we became quite good friends after our study sessions.

So, why did I decide to go up and speak to this gentleman? And what was the uneasy feeling I began to experience when he was telling his story? This is what happens when you try to ignore or disregard one of your values. Sometimes you choose your values; most of the time, your values are already determined by your life experience. Your parents play a huge role in determining your values, and so do your friends and teachers. And then, obviously, a large part of forming our values comes down to our feelings about the world. In this case, I didn't know how compassionate I was toward others, and that value caused me to feel uneasy and sad when that guy told his story. And that value motivated me to do something and try to help. You see, even if we don't realize it, our values help us make decisions every day of our lives. Being compassionate takes little effort, but it can make a massive difference in someone's life. It can help build trust and connection and be a powerful tool for healing and change.

2. Faith

Faith means trusting or believing in something greater than yourself, like religion, philosophy, or a way of life. It can positively affect your mental and physical health. In 2019, Daniela Villani of the Catholic University of the Sacred Heart Milano conducted a study published in Frontiers. She found that people with a strong faith or belief system tend to have lower stress and anxiety levels and report greater overall well-being (Villani, 2019).

This study involved how people's beliefs and spirituality (beliefs in a higher power) affect their happiness and well-being. The study collected data from 267 Italian adults. The study found that people with strong spiritual, philosophical, or religious beliefs have greater overall well-being. This means faith can give you a sense of purpose and direction in life. This sense of purpose will be helpful during challenging and uncertain times. It can also help you foster positive relationships with others, like through a youth group.

You don't necessarily have to believe in God or subscribe to religious beliefs. But don't close yourself off to the possibility of a higher power. Perhaps your God loves all people of the world and wants his believers to do the same. As a Catholic, the peace and happiness my religion gives me is remarkable. But for you, it might be completely different; you might be Hindu, Muslim, Buddhist, Christian, or another religious belief. Suppose you're not a member of any one religious community. In that case, I suggest looking inwards and researching spirituality because we all need to believe in something.

3. Honesty

Honesty means being truthful and trustworthy. In 2011, a study published in the Journal of Experimental Social Psychology by Cynthia S. Wang from the National University of Singapore found that honest people tend to have better relationships with others, including friends, family members, and romantic partners, because honesty creates trust and respect between people (Wang et al., 2011). Additionally, honesty is essential for self-development, as it helps you take responsibility for your actions and make better future decisions. It also helps to build integrity—a value respected by many.

4. Humor

I once felt down and out at a party because I didn't know anyone there. I felt like the only one who wasn't having a good time. I asked myself how I could turn this situation around and try to win some people over?

I began by starting a conversation with one of the other guys who wasn't talking to anyone either. Soon we were having a great conversation, and I was giving my best Chris Rock impression. I told joke after joke and wasn't afraid to laugh at myself when we both realized how bad most of the jokes were. However, the quality of the jokes didn't really matter. People appreciate humor, and by telling a few jokes, the other guy noticed I was trying to be friendly. Soon our laughter attracted the attention of other people at the party. Eventually, my new friend and I were the center of the social sphere—all because I used my humor and wasn't afraid to tell a few jokes. Humor involves finding and making others find amusement in various situations, even difficult ones. It can positively affect your mental health and make you quality friends.

5. Leadership

Leadership means guiding and inspiring others to achieve a common goal. Strong leadership skills can positively affect individuals, groups, and organizations. Leadership can help you develop essential skills like problem-solving, communication, and decision-making, which can benefit many areas of life.

Leadership also helps you to be a role model for others, to inspire, and to make a positive impact on your community. It's important to note that leadership is not only limited to managing a group, but it also means taking the initiative, being responsible for yourself, and influencing and inspiring others toward a common goal.

6. Integrity

Integrity is the adherence to a set of moral and ethical principles. It involves being honest and truthful and having a strong sense of consistency in your actions and values. When I started my business, I was determined to succeed, no matter what it took. I quickly realized, however, that there were certain principles and values I needed to adhere to if I wanted to be successful in the long term. One of the most important of these values for me was integrity.

One of the most challenging situations I faced was when I had to terminate an employee's contract who was not meeting company expectations. It was a difficult decision, but I knew it was right. I was very transparent and honest with the employee, explaining the reasons for the termination. I also took responsibility for my decision and ensured it was done respectfully and professionally. My integrity in that situation helped build trust and respect among my employees, which helped my business succeed. I found that my employees were more engaged and motivated, and my customers appreciated the honesty and transparency I brought to the table.

In addition, my integrity helped me to build strong relationships with suppliers and vendors, which was essential for keeping my business running smoothly. They knew they could trust me to be honest and fair with them, which helped build a sense of loyalty and mutual respect. Integrity is one of the most important values that any business owner can have. It may not always be the easiest path, but it is the one that leads to long-term success and satisfaction.

WHY ARE VALUES IMPORTANT TO OUR LIFE?

Values help us grow as people, give us direction, give our lives meaning, and motivate us. Our values also help us connect with others and build meaningful relationships. When we live in line with our values, we feel happier, more confident, and more successful in our endeavors (What are values and why are they essential? 2021). Remember that values are flexible; they change throughout life, which is normal. Suppose you think back to the fun fact we shared regarding your developing brain. In that case, you won't have a fully developed frontal lobe (the area of the brain in charge of decision-making) until you reach 25. So naturally, your values will change over time as your understanding of the world changes.

Below are tips that will help you understand and identify your values. We will not choose these values for you. Instead, we will set you on the path of self-discovery; at the end, you can identify and determine your values.

You must strive to live by these values, which will help you build a more meaningful life and a successful future.

CHOOSE YOUR VALUES

Here's a step-by-step guide to identifying your values:

Step 1: Reflect on your life and answer some questions

- What inspires you and makes you feel energized in life?
- What qualities do you look for in a partner or friend?
- Summarize yourself in five words?

Step 2: Sort through a list of values

- Look at a list of values and cross out the ones that don't apply to you.
- Keep repeating this process until you are left with 10 values most important to you.
- Write a list of your top 10 values.

Step 3: Determine which values are most important

- Look at your top 10 values and rank them in order of importance.
- Imagine different scenarios and see how they align with your values.
- Reorganize your values in order of importance.

Step 4: Validate your values

- Ask yourself questions to ensure your values align with your life and goals.
- Ask questions like if you would be satisfied with your life if you were described at your funeral using the values you have identified.

- Think about whether you are satisfied with your chosen values and comfortable sharing them with others.

The whole exercise should take less than 30 minutes and is meant to be done on your own with a workbook or paper and pen. It's essential, to be honest throughout the process and to remember that your values can change over time (Values in Life: Practical Exercises to Work Out Your Personal Values, 2019). Now that you have spent time thinking about your values and what's important to you, you will better understand the person you want to be. For example, you may have realized that being honest and respectful is very important to you, and that's something you want to make sure you always strive for in your life.

Discovering your values is a crucial step to becoming your best self. The next step is to put those values into action and constantly work on improving yourself. Moving on to the next chapter, we will discuss developing your social skills. These are the skills that will help you build quality relationships in life!

3

SOCIAL SKILLS

Imagine the following scenario; it's your first day at your new school or college. You're nervous, and everything is so fresh and different. You make it through your first few classes and head to the cafeteria for lunch. You have two options; you can sit alone, or you could sit down at a desk with free space and try to make some new friends. Of course, this is challenging, and everyone would feel awkward in that situation. But thankfully, it doesn't have to be an awkward experience for you. There are plenty of helpful science-backed methods of improving our social skills that will ensure you make long-lasting friendships, no matter where you go. And we will cover all the important ones in this chapter, so if you're looking to brush up on your social skills, this is the one for you.

As a teenager, social skills are particularly important as you navigate the challenges of adolescence and prepare for adulthood. You will need to make new friends, build relationships with romantic partners, and work cooperatively with others in school and the workforce.

What Exactly Are Social Skills?

These skills are how we talk and interact with other people.

This includes not just the words we say but also how we say them and how we use our body language and appearance to communicate (skillsyouneed.com 2011-2023, n.d.-c). The first social skill we will talk about today is arguably the most important skill you can master in life: communication skills. Whether you want to choose a career in the medical, food, energy, teaching, or pharma industry or even run your own business, one thing is certain: good communication skills are essential.

COMMUNICATION

Imagine being stranded on a deserted island with only one person for company. How would you manage your relationship with them? How would you make sure you were both on the same page? This is the importance of communication. It is the key to survival, both physically and emotionally. Without it, you would be lost, alone, and misunderstood. In this section, we are going to explore the art of communication and how it can change your life for the better. Communication skills are like superpowers! They help you talk and share ideas with other people clearly and effectively. Some people are naturally good at communicating, but everyone can learn and practice new communication skills to make their message heard loud and clear. It's like a secret weapon that can make you stand out and be noticed by others (Why Good Communication Skills Are Important for Your Career, 2022).

Perhaps a story would be the most fitting approach to explaining why good communication skills are so important. This one is not about my life exactly; it's about a guy I used to know at university. I first met Seth during one of my physics classes as a freshman. I noticed him at first because whenever the professor would call upon him to answer a question, he would mumble back an answer so quietly that the professor would usually have to ask him to repeat it. From being in the same class and paired up on a few projects, I noticed that Seth was naturally shy and hated speaking in front of the class.

This sucked twice as bad for him because a major part of passing this physics module would involve presenting in front of the entire class on a project we had been working on. I asked Seth how he felt about the presentation, and he said he could hardly bear the thought of getting up in front of the entire class and giving his speech. I nodded and agreed it would be difficult, but thankfully, I had been working as a tour guide and was comfortable in front of crowds. So, after a few weeks, I began preparing for the presentation, as did the rest of my classmates, until, eventually, the big day arrived. Each of us took our turn and gave it our best shot. And soon, it was Seth's turn, and to my amazement, Seth absolutely smashed it! He was so confident up on stage, and he effortlessly communicated his project to the entire class.

Still in shock, I approached Seth after class and asked how in the world he had managed to do that? He smiled, laughed a little, and said he had been practicing for the past semester. When he heard we had to give a presentation, he set aside 15 minutes daily to improve his communication skills. I'll outline some techniques he practiced later in the chapter, but the main thing that stuck with me was how much change was possible from hard work. Here was a guy who was naturally shy and hated the thought of presenting to an entire class, and in just one short semester, he had changed into a wonderful speaker. So, the moral of the story, no matter how poor our communication skills are, we can make incredible improvements by following the tools and exercises outlined in this chapter.

How to Improve Communication Skills

Here are four simple and personalized ways to improve your communication skills:

- Speak clearly and confidently. This means using a clear, steady voice, eye contact, and appropriate body language. To practice, try presenting in front of a mirror or speaking in front of a small group of friends or family.
- Use "I" statements to express your thoughts and feelings. Instead of saying, "You made me angry," try saying, "I feel angry when you do that." This helps to communicate your

feelings without placing blame or causing defensiveness in the other person.

- Learn to manage conflicts effectively. This means learning to identify and express your needs, listening to the other person's perspective, and working together to find a solution. To practice conflict resolution, try role-playing conflicts with a friend or family member or practice identifying and expressing your own needs in real-life conflicts. We will also talk more about conflict resolution later in this chapter.
- Try public speaking. If you want to get better at talking to people and expressing yourself, one of the best things you can do is practice speaking in front of others. It might feel a little scary initially, but the more you practice, the more comfortable you'll get. So, try to find opportunities to talk in front of others, like in class or at a club meeting, and don't be afraid to speak up! (Effective Communication: 6 Ways to Improve Communication Skills - 2023, 2020).

Tips and Tricks for Improving Public Speaking

Strong public speaking skills are the hallmark of a successful man. No matter if you are speaking to your local sports team before a game, talking to a girl in school, or talking during a presentation in school or work. You will be perceived as confident and competent if you can effortlessly communicate your ideas. So, let's look at some methods we can implement to improve our public speaking.

The tips outlined below will help you to improve your public speaking skills:

- Practice diligently: The more you practice speaking in front of an audience, the more comfortable you will become. Try speaking while facing your mirror or to a small group of friends or family. As you become more relaxed, seek out opportunities to speak in front of larger groups, such as at school or community organizations.

- Prepare and plan your speech: Before giving a speech, take the time to prepare and plan what you want to say. Outline the main points you want to make, and practice delivering your speech so it flows smoothly. This will help you feel more confident and in control when giving the speech.
- Use visual aids: Visual aids like slides, pictures, or props can help keep the audience engaged and serve as a helpful reminder for you during the speech. Make sure your visual aids are well-designed and easy to read and practice using them during your preparation.

Exercise for Improving Communication Skills

Practice the exercises below and watch your communication skills improve massively:

- Record yourself speaking: This exercise requires a recording device, like a smartphone or a tape recorder. Start by choosing a topic you are passionate about or find interesting. Record yourself speaking about this topic for 2–3 minutes. After your recording, listen to the playback and focus on your tone, pace, volume, and body language. Identify areas that need improvement, such as filler words, pauses, or gestures, and write them down. Repeat the exercise a few times, focusing on improving one area each time. After each recording, listen to the playback and take notes on your progress. This exercise will help you become more aware of your communication style and how it can be improved. By paying attention to the details of your speech and focusing on improvement, you can refine your skills and become a more effective communicator in personal and professional settings.
- Debate: This can be done in a school debate club or with friends. Choose a topic and research both sides of the argument. Practice communicating your point of view clearly and persuasively. This exercise can help you develop critical thinking and argumentation skills for effective communication.

You've just learned the importance of communication as a social skill, but what happens when things don't go as planned? Conflict can arise in any relationship but can be resolved smoothly with the right tools and mindset. Get ready to learn the art of conflict resolution in the next section and come out on top in any disagreement.

CONFLICT RESOLUTION

You might think, "I have no interest in running my own business." Or "I don't want a cooperate job. Why would I need to practice conflict resolution?" But in truth, we all use our conflict resolution skills daily. Whether with friends, family, girlfriends, bosses, co-workers, or anyone we interact with. Over time and no matter how good your relationship with the person is, eventually, conflict will arise, and you will need to know how to deal with this problem.

Having excellent conflict resolution skills can be the difference between keeping or losing important relationships. Unfortunately, I had to figure this one out myself the hard way. When I was about nineteen, I had a girlfriend I had been with for about two years. We had never really had an argument in the time we had known each other. One day, however, we eventually ended up in an argument, which was a big one! Both of us got extremely angry, and we began shouting at each other. This went on for most of the evening, and then, as most teenage relationships tend to do, we kissed and made up, sweeping the whole argument under the rug. However, the problem with this was that we never really dealt with our problems because we were too angry to effectively resolve the issue. More time passed, and more arguments began to surface until we called it quits on the relationship. I soon realized after this experience that learning how to properly deal with disagreements was a must for my life.

Why Conflict Resolution Is Important for Professional Life

In the story I shared above, you have seen the importance of conflict resolution in our personal lives, but it is just as important for our professional life. Conflict resolution is important for school, college, a job, and business because it helps you get along with others.

When you know how to handle conflicts, you can work through problems and disagreements in a way that's fair for everyone. This can make it easier to get your work done and make friends. It can help you get along better with classmates and teachers in school. In a job, it can help you work better with your colleagues. In business, it can help you make better deals and understand your customers (Why Is Conflict Resolution Important?, 2022).

The tips listed below will help you feel confident in facing conflicts:

- **Listen first**: Before you say anything, hear the other person's side of the story. This will help you understand their perspective, and you might realize that you were wrong (3 Tips to Improve Conflict Resolution Skills, 2017). For example, if your classmate accuses you of not completing your part of the assignment on time, instead of getting defensive, listen to their concerns and ask questions to understand where they are coming from. You may realize that miscommunication or lack of accurate information led to the delay.
- **Agree on the facts**: Make sure you and the other person are on the same page about what happened. This will make it easier to develop a solution (How to Develop Successful Conflict Resolution Skills, 2020). For example, if you and your co-worker disagree on the timeline of events that led to a project delay, ask for specific details and dates to clearly understand the situation.
- **Find the root cause**: Determine what started the problem in the first place. This will help you figure out how to solve it. For example, if you are having a conflict with a loved one about your responsibilities, ask questions to understand the underlying reasons for the disagreement. Was there a lack of communication? Did one party misunderstand the other's expectations? Once you identify the root cause, you can address it and find a solution.
- **Show emotional intelligence**: Be aware of how your words and actions might make the other person feel. Avoid hurtful or personal comments (How to Develop Successful Conflict Resolution Skills 2020). For example, instead of saying "You are wrong" during a

conflict, phrase your disagreement more constructively, such as "I see the situation differently, and here's why."

- **Look for a compromise**: Find a solution where you and the other person are happy. Remember that it's not a competition and that it's possible for both of you to win. For example, if you and your classmate disagree on an assignment and who should have what role, try to find a middle ground by finding a solution that keeps everyone somewhat happy. You rarely find a solution that makes everyone happy, but life is about compromise.

The following exercise will help to improve your conflict resolution skills:

1. Empathy Building Exercise

Think about a conflict or disagreement you had with someone recently. It could be with a friend over who gets to choose the movie to watch or with a family member about who the rightful owner of the last slice of pizza is. In any conflict, it's easy to get wrapped up in our perspective and feelings but taking the time to understand the other person's point of view is a crucial step toward resolving the conflict. You can practice empathy by writing down the details of the situation and your perspective on it. Then, try to put yourself in the other person's shoes in the conflict. Write down their perspective on the situation, including their emotions and thoughts. This exercise can help you understand the other person's point of view and how it can help resolve conflicts in the future.

For example, let's say you had a conflict with a friend over who gets to choose the movie to watch. By taking the time to understand your friend's perspective and how they feel about the situation, you can find a solution that works for both of you, like taking turns choosing the movie or finding a compromise.

2. "I" Statements

Conflicts can often escalate when we blame or accuse the other person involved.

But using "I" statements can help to avoid that and lead to a more productive and respectful conversation. Practice using "I" statements for a few conflicts or disagreements with friends, classmates, or co-workers. You'll find that using "I" statements can help diffuse tension and lead to a better understanding of each other's perspectives. For example, let's say you had a conflict with a classmate about a group project. Instead of blaming them for not contributing enough, you can use "I" statements to express your feelings and needs. You can say, "I feel frustrated because I feel like I'm doing most of the work on the project. Can we work together to find a solution?"

3. Problem-Solving Exercise

Finding a solution that works for both parties is key in any conflict. To practice problem-solving, choose a dispute or disagreement you have had with someone. Note the details of the situation and the issues involved. Then, brainstorm workable solutions to the problem with the other person or alone. Evaluate each solution and choose the one that works best for both parties. For example, let's say you had a conflict with your sibling about who gets to play with the PS5 first. One solution could be to take turns playing with the console or to set a schedule for who gets to play and when. By finding a solution that works for both of you, you can resolve the conflict and avoid similar disagreements in the future.

These exercises can help you develop your conflict resolution skills and improve your relationships with others. By focusing on empathy, effective communication, and problem-solving, you can resolve conflicts constructively and respectfully. Whether it's with friends, family, or co-workers, resolving conflicts effectively can lead to better communication, understanding, and mutual respect. Similar to resolving conflicts, it's important to master the art of active listening. Active listening is the key to understanding someone else's perspective and finding common ground.

It's the foundation of effective communication and an essential tool for conflict resolution. So, let's dive deeper into how to master active listening in the next section!

ACTIVE LISTENING

Simon loved to talk. He would talk to anyone, anytime, about anything. But one day, he realized he was not listening to the people around him while always talking. He didn't understand their perspectives or their feelings. As a result, he often found himself in arguments with his friends and family. Determined to change his ways, Simon embarked on a journey to learn the art of listening. He practiced listening to his friends and family with full attention, without interrupting or judging, and soon he began to understand them better. He started noticing things he never had before, like how his sister was stressed about school or his friend was struggling with a personal problem. He also noticed that the more he listened, the better his relationships became. He was becoming more empathetic, more understanding, and more compassionate. By the end of his journey, Simon had discovered the power of active listening, knowing it was a skill that would serve him well throughout his life.

Active listening is a way of paying attention to someone when they are speaking. It's about trying to understand what the other person is saying instead of waiting for your turn to talk. It is an important social skill (MindTools | Home, n.d.). In 2016, Hadijah and Shalawati from the Universitas Islam Riau published an article in the Journal of English for Academics. The study shows that we spend most of our day communicating, and 40% of this communication consists of listening. They gave students a test and a survey to gather information about their experiences. They found that many students needed help understanding what they were listening to and felt that classes, where they had to primarily listen were the most difficult. They also found that five main things made listening hard for the students: not practicing enough, not having a good vocabulary, understanding native speakers, having trouble with pronunciation, and boring materials. The researchers also found that the students knew it was important to be good at listening, but they needed help from their teachers and other students to improve (Hadijah & Shalawati, 2016).

Listening truly plays such a significant role in our lives. Look at some of the listening stats below:

- Listening is a skill that requires practice. As we age, it becomes increasingly difficult to maintain our focus for extended periods. After just 10 minutes of listening, our attention span drops to 50%. After 48 minutes, it drops even further to 25%. This means we'll likely miss important conversation details without paying close attention.
- It's not just our attention span that's the issue—our mental capacity to listen is also limited. We only use 25% of our mental capacity when listening to someone.
- A school experiment described in Ralph G. Nichols' book found that 90% of children actively listened to their teachers in the first and second grades. However, that number dropped to 44% by middle school, and by high school, it dropped to just 28%.
- It is also important to note that we only remember 17% to 25% of what we listen to. So paying attention to the spoken words, tone of voice, and facial expressions are crucial, as they are responsible for 93% of the message (Tips to Improve Your Active Listening Skills, 2023).

Think about a time when you were in class, and your teacher explained something important. But, instead of paying attention and listening actively, you were busy doodling in your notebook or thinking about something else. Later, when it was time for the test, you realized you didn't understand the material as well as you could have. That's why active listening is so important. When you actively listen, you're not only hearing the words being said but also paying attention to the tone of voice and body language and trying to understand the message (Why Is Active Listening Important for Your Success, 2022).

So next time you're in a class, remember to use your superpower of active listening.

In 2022, an article was published on the Social and Personality Psychology Compass by Netta Weinstein (University of Reading), Guy Itzchakov (University of Haifa), and Nicole Legate (Illinois Institute of Technology). This article talks about how people listening can significantly impact the conversation's outcome. They found that when people listen, they feel in control of the conversation and feel connected to the other person; they are more likely to be open to new ideas and change. The article explains that active listening has been linked to many social, business, and life benefits. These benefits include reduced defensiveness, increased openness and relatability, and motivational change (Weinstein et al., 2022). Below are simple and personalized active listening exercises for you:

1. Limiting Distractions

Okay, so the first thing you must practice in your conversations is limiting distractions. This can be practiced when talking to your family in the morning at breakfast or lunch with your friends in school. Start by turning off your phone and ignoring distractions like noises or TVs. Even if everyone else is on their phones, be the person who tries to spark a conversation and then give it your full attention. Notice their tone, facial expressions, and body language, and focus on the details in their story.

This exercise is a crucial first step in improving your active listening skills. Distractions can prevent you from fully engaging with the person you speak with and understanding their message. Limiting distractions gives the conversation your full attention, allowing you to pick up on important cues, such as tone, facial expressions, and body language, which can give you a better understanding of what the person is trying to say.

2. Reflective Listening Exercise

Reflective listening means understanding what someone is saying and acknowledging their feelings. This type of active listening can help to build trust and strengthen relationships.

Think about a conversation you had with someone recently. Note the conversation's details and the feelings the other person expressed. Then, reflect those feelings to the person by summarizing what you heard. For example, if your friend talked about how stressed they are about school, you could say, "It sounds like you're feeling stressed about school right now."

Reflecting on the other person's feelings demonstrates that you actively listen and care about their experiences. You can use this exercise in school, with your family and friends, or in your future career.

In conclusion, active listening is a vital skill that can significantly impact our relationships—personally and professionally. It involves paying complete attention to the speaker, understanding their message, and responding appropriately. We can improve communication, reduce conflicts, and build stronger relationships by actively listening. Now that we have created the foundation of excellent social skills, we will use them to develop and maintain our relationships. So get ready to take your dating skills to a new level in the next chapter.

4

DATING AND FINDING LOVE

It's perhaps one of man's toughest challenges, finding a woman he is interested in, figuring out if she is interested in him, and then falling in love. Each component of finding a relationship and the complexities once you do are enough to keep any man up at night. And you might not believe me, but everyone has the same irrational thoughts, such as "I'm not good enough to get a girlfriend" or "How could she ever like a guy like me?" These negative thought patterns regarding relationships put a stop to us even trying to find a girlfriend. As the old saying goes, if you're not in it, you can't win it. Meaning nothing will change If you don't make any effort, and I can guarantee you won't find love if you never try. Just remember, life is too short, and we spend so much time worrying about what others will think of us that we often forget to live our own lives.

Thankfully, all those negative thoughts above can be challenged. With some experience (and the expert advice in this chapter), you'll soon have the confidence to walk up to any attractive girl and begin a conversation.

But before we dive deeper into the complicated world of dating, we need to discuss one crucial concept that will not only tie this chapter together but also help us master all of the other skills we have mentioned in the book thus far. And this concept is called exposure therapy.

EXPOSURE THERAPY

You might be thinking, "What is exposure therapy?" Well, let me break it down for you. In the last few chapters, we discussed how important it is to practice and improve your skills, whether the skill is active listening, communication, positive thinking, or conflict resolution. But what happens when fear and anxiety get in the way of practicing these skills? This is where exposure therapy comes in. Exposure therapy is a way of facing your fears and anxieties head-on in a controlled and safe environment. Think about the first time you tried to do something that made you nervous, like speaking to a new friend or girl or giving a presentation. It was probably scary and filled with anxiety, right? But, every time you faced that fear and completed the task, it got easier, and you built confidence, right?

Exposure therapy works similarly. By gradually facing your fears and anxieties, you learn to overcome them and become more confident in your abilities. Now, if you were to read this book in full and think, no way will I ever try to improve my public speaking skill. It's far too scary, or I'm too shy to try and make new friends or talk to a girl, and you decide to ignore the techniques in this book and move on. This guarantees that you stay stagnant and don't improve your life skills. Of course, we know and understand that life's challenges can be tough and sometimes unsurmountable. But the sooner we understand that life is hard and no one will save us but ourselves, we then understand that our lives are truly in our own control.

Exposure therapy is a type of therapy that helps people overcome their fears. When people fear something, they often try to avoid it. But this can make the fear even worse in the long run. That's where exposure therapy comes in.

By gradually exposing yourself to these fears in a safe and controlled way, you can start to feel less scared and avoid them less (What Is Exposure Therapy? 2007). There are a few reasons why exposure therapy works. One is called extinction, which means that after being exposed to the fear many times, the connection between the fear and the physical response (like feeling scared or nervous) starts to weaken. Another reason is habituation, which means that after being exposed to the fear many times, your response to it will weaken until you're no longer afraid (What Is Exposure Therapy & The Benefits | Regain, 2022).

Exposure therapy is effective in helping people overcome various problems, such as:

- Phobias, like a fear of spiders, heights, or public speaking.
- Panic disorder, which is when you have sudden and intense feelings of fear.
- Social anxiety disorder, which is feeling extremely self-conscious and nervous in social situations (social anxiety disorder will make it difficult for you to approach a potential girlfriend).
- Obsessive-compulsive disorder, which is when you have repetitive thoughts and behaviors.
- Posttraumatic stress disorder: a condition that can develop after a traumatic event.
- Generalized anxiety disorder: excessive worry and anxiety about everyday things.

How to Practice Exposure Therapy

Follow the steps below to practice exposure therapy on your own:

Make a List: Write down the things, places, or objects you fear. For example, if you're afraid of dogs, the list could include looking at pictures of dogs, being in the same room as a dog on a leash, and petting a puppy. If you have multiple fears, make different lists for different fear themes.

Create Your Fear Ladder: Rate each item on your list from 0 to 10, with 0 being no fear and 10 being extreme fear. Arrange the listed items from least scary to most scary. This will be your fear ladder.

Facing Fears: Start with the item that causes the least anxiety on your fear ladder. Engage in that activity repeatedly until you start to feel less anxious. If the situation is short, repeat it over and over. If it's longer, stay in the situation long enough for your anxiety to lessen. The longer you face something, the less anxious you'll feel when you face it again. Starting with the least fearful task will help you build confidence, and you will be more ready for the tougher ones. However, if you are already mentally prepared to tackle your biggest fear feel free to begin at the top of the ladder and work down. Often you will find that as you battle to work through the fears at the top of the ladder, as you progress soon, the lower rungs of the fear ladder seem so insignificant that you no longer fear them.

Track Your Progress: Keep track of your fear level during each exposure exercise. Stay in the situation until your fear level drops by about 50%. This way, you'll see your progress and be motivated to keep going.

Gradually Progress: Once you're comfortable with the first item on your fear ladder, move on to the next. Repeat the exposure until you feel comfortable with each item on your fear ladder. With time and practice, you'll be able to face your fears and overcome them (Facing Your Fears: Exposure, n.d.).

Remember, exposure therapy can be very effective if done correctly. So, be willing to try again and follow the steps carefully. Uncover the mysteries of dating in the next section as we delve into the ups and downs of finding a girlfriend. Buckle up for an exciting journey.

DATING

Okay, now, back to the topic at hand, dating. We will outline the best advice we have found during our research and from our personal experience.

But remember, nothing beats practice when it comes to dating and learning to talk to girls. We can give you the best advice, but nothing will change if you don't practice this in real life. Remember, we only regret what we didn't do or say, so don't worry if you fail because it will make you a stronger man, and you'll be more and more confident every time you get out of your comfort zone. Please note that I do not intend to discriminate or offend any individual or community and only present a limited perspective based on my personal experiences. This means even though I speak about relationships between a man and a woman, you can also employ many of these lessons in any relationship.

Dating and the Importance of Relationships

Dating is when you're getting to know someone to possibly have a romantic relationship with them. That's what dating is all about, taking the time to get to know someone and determine if you two are a good match and compatible. Dating has a lot of benefits. Some of them are outlined below:

- You'll live longer because positive relationships reduce stress and encourage healthy habits.
- You'll recover faster from illness or injury because support from a girlfriend lowers stress hormones.
- You'll have lower blood pressure because being in a supportive relationship keeps anxiety at bay.
- Your immune system will be stronger because positive relationships produce more oxytocin, making you less susceptible to stress, anxiety, and depression.
- You'll be more physically fit because the support of a girlfriend can keep you motivated to exercise and eat right.

GETTING A DATE

Here is a step-by-step guide on approaching a girl you like and intending to ask her out.

Remember that this is just a guide to approaching your crush, as everyone will have a different personality. So, with practice, you'll find what works best for you. Okay, it's the big day, and you have finally worked up the courage to ask your crush out. Ensure you check off all these steps and give yourself the best possible chance of getting a date. The first thing you should do before heading to school, work, or college (or wherever you'll see your crush next) is complete an intense workout. Do whatever it takes to get this done. If you need to get up early and run or go to the gym, do it! This will give you an amazing boost in confidence and self-perception, meaning you'll feel relaxed and optimistic, no matter the outcome.

Preparation: Okay, great! You've completed your workout, and now it's time to ensure you look, feel, and smell amazing. Get yourself ready for the day by brushing your teeth and showering. Ensure you are well-groomed and dressed appropriately (we'll discuss hygiene and grooming in detail later in this book). This will give you a boost of confidence and show the girl you care about your appearance.

Find the right time and place: Don't approach the girl during her lunch or when she seems involved in a conversation with someone else. Wait for the right moment when she is alone or in a quiet area where a conversation between you two is possible.

Get the conversation going: This is one of the more challenging parts of the process. It really boils down to how much effort you have put into your communication skills, as beginning and holding a conversation with a lady relies heavily on your communication abilities. If you're not yet the communicator you'd like to be, fear not because this is a perfect place to practice. Here are some things you need to consider:

1. Do you already know this girl?

If you already know her, that's great, as you already know something about her, and you can use this in your conversation.

2. If you don't know her personally, do you have any mutual friends, shared classes, or interests?

These commonalities can also be a great way to kick off and maintain a great conversation. Think along the lines of "Hey, you're such and such's friend" or "Hey, I think we're both in Mr. Ken's trigonometry class."

Asking her out: When the conversation feels natural and you have established a good rapport, you can ask her for a date. Be direct and specific about what you have in mind. For example, you could say, "I was wondering if you would like to see a movie with me this weekend?" or "I was thinking of going for a hike this weekend; would you like to join me?" Be sure to ask respectfully and confidently. If you are both interested in something, this might be a fantastic place to suggest going on a date. Maybe you both like fishing, dining out, or bowling.

Accepting rejection: If the girl says no, handling it with grace and respect is important. Thank her for her time, and let her know that you understand. Remember that rejection is a part of life and doesn't define you. It's important to focus on your self-worth and not let rejection impact your confidence.

Moving forward: Whether the girl says yes or no, it's important to move forward gracefully. If she says yes, congratulations! You can now plan the date and get excited. If she says no, it's important to respect her decision and not pressure her. You can move on and find someone else who is a better fit for you.

In conclusion, asking a girl out on a date can be nerve-wracking. Still, you can make the process much easier with some preparation and confidence. Remember to be respectful, confident, and direct, and you'll have a better chance of getting the outcome you're hoping for. Suppose she says yes; the next section will help you plan a fun and thoughtful date that fits your interests and preferences.

WHAT TO DO NOW THAT YOU HAVE A DATE

So, you finally mustered up the courage to ask that special girl out, and she said yes! Time to plan your first date.

Don't stress; I've got you covered. I've gathered the best tips, backed by science and personal experience, to make your date successful. I remember the first time I had a date with someone I liked. I was nervous and excited and had no idea what to expect. I felt like I had reached the next level but realized I didn't know what the next level entailed.

1. Pick the Right Location

The place to go is a neutral, low-pressure spot where you can focus on getting to know each other. A local coffee shop works great. You can always leave after the first drink if it's not going well or continue if it is.

2. Engage in a Great Conversation

Skip the cheesy pick-up lines and opt for interesting topics. Ask questions that show you're curious and intelligent. Try these:

- If you could be anything when you grow up, what would it be?
- What's your favorite kind of music?
- What would be a perfect day for you?
- Tell me about your family?
- Do you want to attend college, and what college do you plan on attending?

All these questions are not only great conversation starters, but you can also learn a lot about her values and if you have a shared (or at least similar) outlook on the world. These questions also allow you to respond with your own answers, and it's a great chance to show her who you are.

3. Think about the Past but Don't Dwell on It

Don't dwell on the negative if you've had bad dating experiences. Think about what you can learn from them instead. Did you act in a mean or unfair way during your dates?

Is there anything you could have done differently to make the situation better? A crucial skill or concept to learn is the thought that everything in your life, good and bad, is partly or fully your fault.

Whether this holds true for every one of your life's situations or not, it can be helpful to think this way. Now, obviously, horrible things happen to people, such as illness or abuse, and this is not their fault. That's not what we are speaking of here. This concept only covers certain things in life, such as whether you passed a math test, got that promotion at work, or managed to get that girl's number? Often when we receive bad news or face rejection, our first thought is to blame someone else. We could say, "Oh, my teacher or boss hates me. That's why I didn't get promoted." Or "That girl didn't give me her number because she is mean." If you have this mindset where you blame others, you give them control, and nothing will change. But if you take the blame and responsibility, your mind will begin to look for solutions, and you can improve as you are in control.

4. Body Language Matters

Here's a personal story: I was on a date with a girl and was nervous. I didn't realize I was crossing my arms until she pointed it out. I changed it, leaned in, and started mirroring her movements. It made all the difference; she told me how much she appreciated my attentiveness. Your body language speaks louder than your words on a date. And it's not always easy to control, but small changes can make a big difference. Here's what to watch out for:

- **Show Interest**: Tilt your head, lean in, and avoid crossing your arms when your date is talking. These nonverbal cues show you're paying attention and want to hear more.
- **Read Them**: Check your date's body language for similar cues. If they're crossing their arms or facing away from you, it might be time to change the subject.
- **Mirroring**: We mimic the behaviors of people we're attracted to. It's a subtle way to show interest. So, try to do the same if your date shifts or smiles.

- **Fronting**: When you face your entire body toward your date, it shows engagement. But if their toes are pointed toward the exit, it might not be a great sign.
- **Leaning**: If your date leans toward you, they're attracted and want to be closer. If they sit back or step away, they might not feel connected (Science-Backed First Date Tips To Make Your Date Great, 2023).

5. Be Interested

Want to impress your date and show off your awesome self? It's simple, be interested in them! Everyone loves talking about themselves, so ask your date questions about them. You'll show that you care, and that makes you more interesting. No one likes a show-off, but being curious is cool. ***Tip***: A personal story always makes things more interesting. Share one to show your date a fun side of you.

6. Be Yourself on a Date

Dating can feel like a contest, but it doesn't have to be. Finding someone you connect with and who makes you happy matters. Being true to yourself is key to finding that special someone.

7. Follow Up After a Great First Date

So, you had a great time on your first date. Now what? A successful first date needs a follow-up to keep the connection going. Send a message soon after to say you had a great time and suggest another meet-up. Don't be too eager or pushy. Just be confident (First Date Tips: How to Have a Successful First Date the Blue Ocean Way, 2023).

So, there you have it. With these tips, you're ready to rock your first date. Good luck, and have fun! But what comes next? If you are a good match for one another and enjoy each other's company, then you might want to make her your girlfriend. The next section will dive into tips and tricks to make your girl feel loved and appreciated. I'll show you how to take your relationship to the next level. So, buckle up and get ready to become the best boyfriend you can be!

HOW TO BE THE PERFECT BOYFRIEND

After I started dating, I realized being in a relationship was more challenging than I thought. I made countless mistakes and often wondered what I could do to be a better boyfriend. It was not until I learned from my own experiences and reflections that I discovered the key to being the perfect boyfriend. I want to share invaluable lessons about relationships and how to be the perfect boyfriend. This is how I learned to listen, compromise, and always make rational decisions. Trust me; it's not rocket science. Anyone can do it with little effort. Here are the things you need to keep in mind:

1. Attention

Girls love to talk and want someone to listen to them without being bored or tuning out. If you want to show her that you care, give her your full attention, and listen to what she has to say.

2. Space

It's important in a relationship to give each other some space and not be attached at the hip all the time. Just because you're in a relationship doesn't mean you own each other. Letting her pursue her interests and have time with friends can strengthen your relationship. When you have separate social lives and hobbies, you have something interesting to discuss when you're together again. It helps you both maintain a sense of individuality. Don't force her to like all the same things as you, and make sure to keep up the hobbies and interests you had before the relationship. This way, you can grow separately and together in love, leading to a strong relationship (How to Become a Better Husband, Boyfriend, or Life Partner, 2020).

3. Sense of humor

Making her laugh and showing her the lighter side of life can bring a smile to her face and make you both feel good. Plus, she'll see you as not just a boyfriend but also a friend.

4. Honesty

Women want someone they can trust, so being honest is key. You can show her you're honest by being punctual, following through on your promises, and being truthful about your feelings.

5. Respect

No matter how independent or strong a woman is, they all want to be treated respectfully. This means caring about her feelings, supporting her, and not playing games with her. However, the same goes for you also. Make sure you find a woman who respects you as a person, as those are the relationships that last.

6. Compromise

When it comes to relationships, compromise is key. Imagine you and your girlfriend disagree about what movie to watch on date night. Instead of fighting, you sit and talk calmly about each other's preferences. It's important to remember that compromising doesn't mean one person always wins and the other always loses. You both need to take turns making decisions that work for both of you. For example, she picks the movie, and you choose the dinner spot (3 Ways to Be a Good Boyfriend). By following these tips, you'll be on your way to being the perfect boyfriend. Good luck!

In conclusion, finding love can be a wild ride but ultimately worth it. Remember to communicate, compromise, add a touch of spontaneity, and give each other space. All of these things will help keep the fire burning in your relationship. But before reaching that point, you must ensure you're presenting your best self. In the next chapter, we'll dive into the importance of personal hygiene, grooming, and fashion. Because let's face it, you can't expect someone to love you if you don't love yourself first. So, prepare to up your game and look your best because finding love starts with you!

5

PERSONAL HYGIENE, GROOMING, AND FASHION

Have you ever walked into a room and felt embarrassed because of your appearance? In college, I remember showing up to my chemistry class with a huge zit on my chin, greasy hair, and wrinkled clothes more suited to a jog around campus rather than attending a lecture. My classmates snickered, and I felt so self-conscious that I couldn't focus on the professor's words. That day, I realized the importance of personal hygiene, grooming, and fashion. It's not just about looking good but also about feeling confident and ready to face the world. I vowed never to be embarrassed about my appearance or fashion sense again and began to discover how men are supposed to dress and present themselves. This chapter will dive into the significance of these three crucial things: hygiene, grooming, and fashion.

PERSONAL HYGIENE

Personal hygiene includes keeping your body clean and healthy for your physical and mental well-being. It also has the added bonus of making people want to hang out with you, as a person who looks and smells great is very attractive (Why is personal hygiene important? 2020). Personal hygiene is important to you for the following reasons:

Keep Diseases at Bay:

Did you know your hands encounter bacteria when touching things like your pet, a doorknob, or your face after sneezing? Those germs can multiply and make you sick if you don't wash up regularly. But don't worry; washing your hands and body can eliminate those pesky germs and help you remain healthy! And not only will good hygiene keep you healthy, but it'll also keep others around you healthy. No one likes being near someone with bad breath or body odor, right? By keeping yourself clean, you'll avoid spreading germs and make everyone's day a little better (What Are the Benefits of Good Personal Hygiene? 2022).

Be Popular and Professional:

Good hygiene can also significantly impact your social and professional life. Not only will people want to be around you more, but employers will also take notice. They want to hire people who look and smell clean and take their health seriously, especially if they work in the food or medical industry. And let's not forget about the playground. Did you know that poor hygiene is one of the main reasons kids get bullied at school? By practicing good hygiene, you can avoid becoming a target and have more friends.

Feel Confident and Radiant:

Feeling clean and well-groomed can give you a huge boost of confidence and make you feel physically and mentally better. On the other hand, if you don't practice good hygiene, you might feel uncomfortable, irritable, and anxious.

Avoid Pain and Suffering:

Did you know that not brushing and flossing can lead to gum disease and tooth loss? Yikes! Good hygiene can also help you avoid athlete's foot and other painful conditions, so wash up and take care of yourself (Good Hygiene, 2020).

How to Take Care of Your Personal Hygiene Needs

Bathe regularly: This means taking a shower or a bath at least once daily to keep your body clean and fresh. This helps remove dirt, sweat, and oils that can build up on your skin and cause bad odor. After every workout, a shower is also necessary to remove excess sweat.

Wash your hands: This is one of the simplest and most effective ways to prevent the spread of germs and bacteria. You should wash your hands with soap and water for at least 20 seconds, especially after using the bathroom, blowing your nose, coughing, or sneezing.

Trim your nails: Keeping your nails trimmed and clean helps prevent the growth of bacteria and germs under your nails. You should trim your nails regularly and clean them with a nail brush.

Brush and floss: Brushing your teeth twice a day and flossing at least once a day helps keep your mouth clean and free of bacteria. This can prevent bad breath and tooth decay, keeping your smile bright and healthy!

Sleep: Sleeping is important for overall health, including hygiene. Aim for 8–9 hours of sleep each night to help your body recharge and rejuvenate.

Take care of your skin: It is your body's largest organ, and keeping it healthy and hydrated is important. This means using a gentle cleanser, moisturizing regularly, and wearing sunblock when you go outside. Caring for your skin can help prevent dryness, wrinkles, and skin damage. The sun is amazing for us, but too much-unprotected sun exposure can leave you looking much older than you are (A Guide to Good Personal Hygiene, 2009).

Acne: If you suffer from acne, there are several things you can do to combat this issue. First, consult a dermatologist who can help you with your individual case, as the cause of each person's acne can differ. Aside from this, there is a lot you can do yourself at Home. First, try eliminating dairy products from your diet. Dairy products are filled with hormones that can cause your skin to become oilier, clog pores, and increase inflammation, all pointing to a no-go for people with acne. The same goes for sugar. Try eliminating it from your diet, as the inflammation caused by sugar can lead to breakouts. Try to wash your face at night with a good cleanser and moisturize, as this will prevent your skin from getting too oily. Also, consider trying a low-carbohydrate diet, as this has been shown to work miracles for fighting acne. Of course, check with your doctor to see if this diet could work for you. But from personal experience, I can say it worked wonders for my skin. Following these simple steps can keep your body clean, healthy, and feeling great!

Hygiene Tips for the Private Areas of the Body

Keeping your private parts clean and healthy is super important! When it comes to intimate hygiene for guys, many think it's only about sexual health and wellness. But it's about so much more than that! Poor intimate hygiene can lead to smelly situations, itching, sweating, rashes, and pimples. That's why taking care of your private area is key to keeping your overall health and fitness on point. The area around your groin has more sweat glands than other parts of your body, so having a good intimate hygiene routine is especially important. Washing in the shower is just the beginning. There are many other tips to help keep your private area healthy, some of which are outlined below. Giving your intimate parts a daily shower is a must! Make sure to wash your penis, scrotum, anus, and pubic hair daily with water (be careful of using harsh soaps or shower gels as they can cause irritation).

Some Hygiene Hacks

A great life hack for smelling your best is to apply your aftershave or deodorant to pulse points on your body, like your wrists, neck, and inner elbows.

These areas generate heat throughout the day, which helps to release the fragrance. Another tip is to wait a few minutes after showering to apply your aftershave or deodorant. This allows your skin to dry completely and ensures the fragrance sticks better and lasts longer. Additionally, you can layer your fragrance using scented body lotion or wash before applying the aftershave or deodorant. This will create a longer-lasting scent and help you smell your best all day!

In conclusion, personal hygiene is vital to maintaining good health and well-being. Regular bathing, handwashing, and oral care are just some of the many ways to ensure you take care of your hygiene. Proper personal hygiene keeps you clean and protects you from harmful germs and bacteria that can lead to various health issues. In the next section, we will discuss grooming, another important aspect of personal hygiene. Grooming involves taking care of your physical appearance. It is essential to keep yourself well-groomed to maintain a positive self-image and to feel confident and comfortable in social situations.

GROOMING

Growing up, I always thought grooming was a routine performed by women only. When I started working in a fast-paced corporate environment, I realized grooming was just as crucial for men. The first time I went to a barber, I was shocked by the attention and care taken to make me look good. I felt like a new person, from a fresh shave to a precise haircut. That experience opened my eyes to men's grooming and how it can greatly impact confidence and appearance. In this chapter, I will teach you everything I picked up along the way. Prepare to open doors and make an impact with a polished and poised look!

Grooming is taking care of yourself and ensuring you look and feel your best. It's not just about showering and brushing your teeth. It's about taking pride in your appearance and showing the world the best version of yourself. Think about it—when you take the time to groom yourself, you feel more confident and ready to take on the day.

Whether it's getting a fresh haircut, trying out new skincare products, or even just brushing your hair, these small steps can impact your overall confidence (What Is Men's Personal Grooming?, 2020). So, try out that new haircut you've been eyeing, and remember, taking care of yourself is always worth it. Male grooming is not just about looking good. It's about feeling good too. You only get one chance to make a first impression, and grooming can play a big role. Imagine walking into a job interview with messy and unkempt hair and a scruffy beard. It might not make the best impression on the interviewer. On the other hand, taking a little time to groom yourself, like getting a fresh haircut, and trimming your beard, can make you feel more confident and ready to tackle anything. Plus, when you look good, you feel good! And who doesn't want to feel good every day? So, whether you're going on a date, hanging out with friends, or running errands, make sure you take the time to groom yourself and show the world the best version of yourself. Below is the best grooming advice for your hair, skin, and facial hair:

Hair:

Get a haircut regularly to maintain the shape and style you desire. Invest in a good hairstyling product like gel, pomade, or wax to keep your hair in place all day. Treat your hair to a hair mask or deep conditioner at least once weekly to keep it healthy and nourished.

Skin:

Cleanse your face every day to remove dirt and oil build-up. Moisturize your skin to prevent dryness and maintain a healthy complexion. Use a toner to balance your skin's pH and keep it healthy.

Facial Hair:

When the time comes to shave, use a good quality razor and shaving cream to prevent irritation. Invest in a good pair of scissors and comb for beard trimming to keep your beard neat. Use beard oil or balm to keep your beard soft and hydrated (The Ultimate Guide To Men's Grooming, 2022).

Note: As a teenager, you may not be using all these grooming products or techniques yet, but it's important to know about them to prepare when the time comes. By caring for yourself now, you'll set yourself up for a lifetime of good grooming habits.

In a 2009 study published in the science direct journal by French & Robins et al., some amazing findings came out surrounding personal appearance and male grooming and how they affected the GPA (Grade Point Average) of high schoolers. The study set out to test both male and female students. Aspects like attractiveness, grooming, and personality were then measured alongside the student's GPAs. Amazingly, the male students who paid the closest attention to their grooming had a statistically higher GPA than those who did not (French & Robins et al. (2009)).

This shows the power grooming can have on the rest of our lives. Suppose we introduce discipline into our lives with something like grooming. In that case, it can lead to discipline in other things like schoolwork, sporting endeavors, work, or dating girls. So, apply this to your life and see what it can bring you. Step up your grooming game and boost your confidence! An excellent grooming routine makes you feel good about yourself and positively impacts how others perceive you. Show the world that you're confident and capable, which can lead to many opportunities in your personal life and career.

In conclusion, male grooming is a crucial aspect of personal care. It can positively impact your appearance, confidence, and overall self-image. Regular grooming helps you look and feel your best and leaves a lasting impression on others. Following a consistent routine that includes basic hygiene practices and grooming habits is important. Now that we've covered the basics of male grooming let's move on to the exciting world of fashion!

Fashion is an art form that allows individuals to express themselves and showcase their style. Get ready to dive into the trends that will have you looking your best!

FASHION

Fashion is a way of expressing yourself through your clothes and accessories. It's about finding your style and being confident.

Whether staying up to date with the latest trends or creating a unique look, fashion is all about having fun and showing the world who you are.

A Brief History of Men's Fashion

Men's fashion has undergone many changes throughout history, with different styles becoming popular in different eras. In the 1800s, men's fashion was characterized by a more formal and conservative look. This was when waistcoats, cravats, and top hats were considered essential for a gentleman's wardrobe. As the 1900s approached, men's fashion became more relaxed and casual, reflecting the more laid-back attitudes of the time. During World War I, men's fashion became more practical and functional, as soldiers needed comfortable and durable clothing.

The 1920s saw a resurgence in men's fashion with the introduction of jazz and the flapper culture. Suits became more fitted and fashionable, and accessories such as fedoras and suspenders became popular. The 1930s and 1940s were characterized by the Great Depression and World War II, and men's fashion reflected the more serious and practical attitudes of the time. The 1950s and 1960s saw a revival in men's fashion, with the introduction of the "dandy" look and the popularity of the Ivy League style. The 1970s and 1980s were a time of great change in men's fashion. New materials and styles, like bell bottoms and leisure suits, were becoming popular.

Today, men's fashion is more diverse and eclectic than ever before. From streetwear to traditional suits, there is a style for every taste and occasion.

With the advent of technology and the internet, men's fashion has become more accessible and more democratic, allowing anyone to express themselves through the clothes they wear (A Brief History of Men's Fashion, n.d.).

What Benefits Can Fashion Provide You

Dressing well can have a significant impact on your life, and here are a few of the benefits you can expect as a teenager and as a man:

Boosts Confidence: Wearing clothes that you feel comfortable and good in can make you feel more confident in any situation, whether in school, a job interview, or a social gathering.

Improves First Impressions: People tend to form first impressions based on how someone looks, and dressing well can help you make a great first impression on others.

Increases Opportunities: Wearing professional attire can make you stand out positively and increase your chances of success in both your personal and professional life.

Shows Respect: When you dress nicely, you respect the people you are meeting or the event you attend.

Boosts Self-Esteem: Feeling good about your appearance can boost your self-esteem and make you more positive and motivated.

Indicates Success: Wearing well-fitted and stylish clothes can indicate that you are successful, which can help open doors for you professionally and personally. It's worth finding what styles work best for you and building a wardrobe that makes you feel confident and ready for anything. Here are some key takeaways for teenage boys looking to improve their fashion sense:

Invest in quality basics: A few high-quality essentials like plain t-shirts, jeans, and sneakers can go a long way in creating a stylish outfit. These items should fit well and be made of durable materials.

Experiment with patterns and colors: Don't be afraid to try bold patterns and bright colors.

A graphic tee or a printed shirt can add interest to a simple outfit.

Invest in outerwear: A good jacket or coat can significantly impact your style. Look for pieces that are both warm and fashionable.

Accessorize: Accessories like a watch, belt, or sunglasses can elevate your look. Choose items that match your style and that you feel comfortable wearing.

Pay attention to fit: Fit is key when it comes to fashion. Ensure your clothes fit you well and aren't too baggy or tight.

Dress for the occasion: Consider where you're going and what you'll be doing when choosing your outfit. Dressing appropriately shows respect for the event and makes you look more put together.

Build a versatile wardrobe: Focus on creating a wardrobe with pieces that can be mixed and matched to create multiple outfits. This will make getting dressed in the morning easier and save you money in the long run (Essential rules every well-dressed man should know, 2022).

Fashion is about expressing yourself and having fun. Try different styles and see what works best for you. You'll get better at it over time, and in a few years, you'll be ready to step up your game even more! According to a study published in the Princeton School of International Affairs by B. Rose Kelly from Princeton University in 2019, how someone is dressed can greatly impact how others perceive them. The study found that people who dress well are perceived as more competent and authoritative than those who dress more casually or in a sloppy manner (Kelly, 2019).

The same is said in an article published in the Journal of Human Behavior in 2019. This article was published by DongWon Oh from New York University. The study found that how you dress can make a big difference in how people see you. People who dress nicely, with clean and well-fitting clothes, are seen as more competent, trustworthy, and attractive (Oh, 2019). This is important for you, especially if you want to make a good impression on others at school or in the future. So, think about what you wear and try to dress nicely.

In conclusion, personal hygiene, grooming, and fashion are crucial in making a positive first impression and maintaining good health. Regular grooming and adopting a well-maintained appearance can enhance your confidence and self-esteem. The next chapter will delve into building a healthy body that will keep us healthy and massively increase our attractiveness to others.

6

HEALTHY LIVING

Our bodies are like a house we will have to live in for the next 70–80 years, so why not look after them? Unfortunately, we see more of the opposite happening in today's world. Obesity is at an all-time high in the U.S., chronic illnesses in the teenage population have increased dramatically in the previous decades, and teen mental health is in poor condition. But why is this—can't there be a better way to live? I believe that many of our problems today as teens boil down to an unhealthy lifestyle, so why not make the change today?

Personally, health and longevity (living a long life) have always been major interests of mine, so I have always enjoyed researching these topics over the years. In this chapter, you'll find all the best advice I have accumulated. So please, if you find something you think could benefit your life or your health, take note, and of course, feel free to email me with any questions (our email is at the back of the book).

SLEEP AND THE SCIENCE BEHIND IT

You know how sometimes you feel tired and ready for bed, and other times you feel wide awake and ready to take on the world?

That's all thanks to your body clock! It's like a 24-hour timer in your body that tells you when it's time to feel tired or when it's time to be awake. This is called your circadian rhythm. And the reason you get tired in the first place is because of a chemical called adenosine. The more you stay awake, the more adenosine your brain makes, making you sleepy. But when you sleep, your body breaks down the adenosine, which makes you feel more alert when you wake up.

Light also plays a big role in your body clock. Your brain has a special part called the hypothalamus, the control center that keeps track of when it's light or dark outside. If it's getting dark, your brain releases a hormone called melatonin that makes you feel sleepy. But when the sun rises, your body releases a hormone called cortisol, which gives you energy and makes you feel awake (Why Do We Need Sleep? 2022).

Importance of Sleep to Your Health

Did you know your brain does amazing things when you're asleep? It helps consolidate memories, boosts mood, and even improves problem-solving skills. Getting enough sleep can make you smarter! But that's not all. Getting enough sleep can also help you:

Maintain a healthy weight: Lack of sleep is linked to increased hunger and cravings for junk food as Ghrelin (hunger hormone) levels in the blood increase.

Improve your athletic performance: Sleep helps your body recover from physical activity, so getting enough sleep can help you perform better in sports or other physical activities.

Boost your immune system: Sleep helps your body fight illness and infection.

Reduce stress: Sleep is a natural way to help your body manage stress.

Improve your mood: Lack of sleep is linked to irritability, anxiety, and depression (M. P. Therapy, 2021).

So, as a teenager, it's super important to ensure you're getting enough sleep each night.

Aim for 8–9 hours of quality sleep every night, and you'll be on your way to a healthier, happier life! In 2022, Qiman Jin and six other scientists published an article in Epidemiology and Social Inequalities in Health. They wanted to see if there was a connection between how much sleep people get and their risk of dying from heart disease or all-cause mortality. They looked at information from an extensive survey in the U.S. that happened from 2005 to 2014, and they followed up with those people until the end of 2015 to see who had died.

They used statistical analyses to figure out how much of a risk people had based on how much sleep they got and other aspects about them, like how old they were and if they smoked. They found that people who slept less than 5 or more than 9 hours a day were likelier to die from all-cause mortality and heart disease. It turns out that a lot of heart disease could be prevented if people slept the right number of hours (Jin et al., 2022).

Another study explored the connection between sleep, overall well-being, and the academic performance of college students at the National University of Singapore. The study looked at different aspects of sleep, such as how long they slept, sleep quality, how often they had sleep problems, daytime tiredness, and how long it took them to fall asleep. The researchers also measured the student's academic performance using their grade point average (GPA) and well-being using two different assessments. The results showed that sleep quality directly impacted the students' overall well-being and academic performance (Armand, 2021).

How to Improve Sleep

You may improve your sleep in various ways, beginning with developing a consistent sleep routine. Try to have a regular sleep/wake schedule, even on weekends. This aids in regulating your body's internal clock, making it simpler to fall asleep and wake up feeling refreshed. Creating a peaceful evening routine is another approach to improving your sleep.

Avoid using electronic devices, like phones and computers, 1–2 hours before bed because the blue light emitted by these gadgets might disrupt your sleep. Instead, read a book or listen to relaxing music before bed. You can also make your bedroom more soothing by keeping it cool, dark, and quiet. Make sure your bed is comfortable. You can dramatically increase the quality of your sleep by creating a sleep-friendly environment and sticking to a consistent sleep routine (Good Sleep Habits, 2022).

In conclusion, sleep is like a magical potion for your body! It helps you recharge, refresh, and feel ready to tackle the day ahead. When you get enough sleep, you are less grumpy, more focused, and creative, your immune system is stronger, and you even look better! So, make sure you get enough sleep every night. Let's move on to the next important aspect of healthy living—exercise! Just like sleep, exercise has many benefits for your body and mind. Get ready to learn how moving your body can help you feel amazing!

EXERCISE AND ITS BENEFITS FOR HEALTHY LIVING

Exercise is like the ultimate body and mind update! It's like pressing the supercharge button, igniting a rush of fantastic advantages. Moving your body makes you feel more energized and less stressed—a significant benefit in today's fast-paced world. A few minutes of exercise can improve your mood and make you feel better, so think about what you can accomplish with a full workout!

But hold on; there's more! Exercise makes you appear and feel stronger, and it's a great way to boost your confidence. When you physically challenge yourself, you are also developing mental toughness. Furthermore, exercise helps you sleep better. When you get enough sleep, you're more focused, creative, and ready to handle Anything that comes your way (Benefits of Physical Activity, 2022). But here's the thing: exercise isn't just beneficial for looking good; it's also good for your health. According to the World Health Organization, regular physical activity can reduce the risk of severe diseases like heart disease, stroke, type 2 diabetes, and certain types of cancer by up to 50%. Exercise will not only make you feel great, but it will also help you live a longer and healthier life!

Scientific Studies Showing the Importance of Exercise

In 2006, Darren Warburton from the University of British Columbia published an article in the Canadian Medical Association Journal. This article reviews different studies about the impact of exercise on our health. The author wanted to see how physical activity affects our health and if it can prevent serious illnesses like heart disease, diabetes, cancer, high blood pressure, depression, and osteoporosis. The study found that exercise is fantastic for our health and can prevent these illnesses and even death (Warburton, 2006). The study also found that the more we exercise, the better our health will be.

The benefits of exercise were also shown by another study in 2016. Tayyeb Taher Zade (Islamic Azad University) and two others published this article in Trends in Life Sciences. The study was conducted to see if exercise can make young people feel better about themselves, happier, and improve their overall life. Sixty people just starting to work out at a gym in Darab city were chosen to participate in the study. They were compared to 60 people of the same age, gender, and education level but who didn't exercise. The study participants worked out for three months, three times a week for 1 hour. They took surveys about their self-esteem, happiness, and quality of life before and after the study. The results showed that the people who exercised felt better about themselves, were happier and had a better overall life (Zade et al., 2015).

This indicates that exercise is a good way to improve physical and mental health without causing any harm. Below are some exercises that you can try:

Aerobic exercises: Aerobic exercises are great for your heart and lungs. They include running, jogging, cycling, swimming, and even dancing. Start with 5–10 minutes of aerobic exercise and gradually increase the duration and intensity as you get fitter.

Strength training: Strength training is important for building muscle and improving bone density. You can try bodyweight exercises like push-ups, squats, and lunges or use resistance bands or dumbbells. Start with lighter weights and focus on good form and proper technique.

Stretching: Stretching can help to improve flexibility and reduce the risk of injury. Try stretching each major muscle group for 10–15 seconds, then repeat 2–3 times.

Yoga: Yoga is a great form of exercise that can help to improve strength, flexibility, balance, and focus. Start with a beginner yoga class or find a beginner yoga video online.

Always warm up before you start exercising and cool down after you finish. This can help to prevent injury and reduce muscle soreness. Also, drink plenty of water before, during, and after exercise to stay hydrated. In summary, exercise can significantly improve your physical and mental health as a teenager. Try different exercises to see what you enjoy the most, and warm up, cool down, and stay hydrated. Now let's see how important diet is to healthy living.

DIET

Eating healthy is super important for keeping yourself happy, healthy, and feeling good. This means eating different types of food in the right amounts and making sure you consume the right amount of food and drink to stay at a healthy weight (NHS website, 2023).

We'll look at a healthy diet in this section. Please note that this advice is for everyone in general. If you have any special needs or health problems, you should talk to a doctor or a dietitian for help.

What Makes Up a Healthy Diet?

A healthy diet includes a variety of delicious and nutritious foods, including:

Fruits and veggies: Apples, bananas, carrots, and spinach! These are packed with vitamins and minerals that your body needs.

Whole grains: Whole wheat bread and oatmeal. These are a good source of fiber and will keep you full for longer.

Lean protein: Go for chicken, fish, tofu, and legumes. This helps build and repair your muscles.

Dairy or dairy alternatives: Milk, cheese, and yogurt (or non-dairy alternatives like almond milk) are good sources of calcium and other important nutrients.

Healthy fats: Avocados, nuts, and seeds are all great choices. They provide energy and help your body absorb vitamins.

Benefits of a Healthy Diet

Eating healthy is like fueling your body with the right food and drink. Just like a car needs high-quality gasoline to run smoothly, your body needs nutritious food to work at its best and keep you feeling great. A healthy diet can give you energy, boost your mood, and even help you stay focused in school. It can also protect you from diseases and illnesses, keep your skin and hair looking good, and help you maintain a healthy weight. Think of your body as a engine; eating healthy is like offering it the best sacrifices to keep it strong, healthy, and glowing. So, if you want to feel your best, look your best, and live a happy and healthy life, a balanced and nutritious diet is the way to go!

Tips for Eating Healthy

First, make sure you're eating the right amount of food for how active you are.

You'll gain weight if you eat too much because your body will store the extra food as fat. And if you eat too little, you'll lose weight. An important rule here is calories in vs. calories out. For example, suppose your daily calorie needs are 2,700 calories, and you consume fewer calories. In that case, you will lose weight, but if you consume more calories than you have burned, you'll gain weight. Eating various foods is essential, so your body gets all the necessary nutrients. Ensure you eat fiber-rich carbohydrates like whole wheat pasta, rice, and potatoes. These will help you feel full for longer.

You should also eat five portions of fruit and vegetables every day! This can be fresh, frozen, canned, dried, or juiced. Just limit sugary drinks like fruit juice and be aware of fruit smoothies. Once you blend fruit and consume it, it affects your body differently than eating it whole, as the sugars are more readily available to your body. Eat fish twice a week, including at least one portion of oily fish like salmon, as it's a good source of protein and nutrients like omega-3 fatty acids.

Try to eat less saturated fat and sugar. Saturated fat can raise cholesterol levels, which can harm your heart. Instead of vegetable oils, use a small amount of olive oil or grass-fed butter, and choose lean cuts of meat. Finally, limit foods and drinks high in sugar as they can lead to weight gain and tooth decay. In fact, the more sugar you remove from your diet, the healthier and longer your life will be, as it is truly bad for our bodies and mind. These tips will help you make healthier food choices and keep your body happy and healthy! Sleep, exercise, and diet are not the only ways to achieve healthy living. Certain therapies, like cold water therapy, can help you become healthier.

Cold Water Therapy

People on Instagram love to post videos of themselves getting into freezing cold water, like ice baths or jumping into a cold lake. Even though it may seem like a silly trend, this is an old practice called "cold water therapy." This is when you use cold water to make your body healthier or help with an injury or illness. It's been around for a long time and is used to help injuries heal faster, reduce muscle and joint pain, and get you back to feeling better after working out.

People from different cultures have been using cold water therapy for millennia to stay healthy. A long time ago in Rome, people used to soak in cold water to relax and feel better. Roman doctor Claudius Galen even recommended it for treating fevers! In the early 1900s, a doctor named Edgar A. Hines did some research to understand how cold water affects the body. He discovered that it could change how your blood pressure works and affect your "autonomic nervous system," which controls things like your heart rate.

In recent years, scientists have been looking into how cold water can help you recover after exercising. They've found that it helps improve circulation and can help with muscle damage and soreness. That's why many athletes, both professional and not, use cold water therapy to recover after working out. Cold water therapy is frequently used in physical therapy to relieve pain and reduce inflammation in chronic and acute pain. Consider it a boost for your body! Cold water therapy might temporarily improve your mood. Cold water immersion has been shown in studies to enhance dopamine levels, a hormone that enhances mood, by a whopping 250% (What to Know About Cold Water Therapy, 2920).

With so many amazing benefits, it's easy to see why so many people are turning to cold water therapy. Lowering the body's inflammation is great, and if you're an athlete having less muscle soreness is always a plus. One thing to watch out for here is to avoid cold water exposure directly after a resistance training session. Your muscles need the inflammation caused by the workout to break down and repair the muscle, causing them to grow. So, taking an ice bath after a squat session will lower the workout's effectiveness. Instead, if you plan on having an ice bath that day, take it before the workout, as this can increase your testosterone. Plus, if you are struggling with stress, anxiety, or depression, the huge dopamine boost it can give you for the day is wonderful for the mind.

How to Practice Cold Water Therapy

Buying expensive equipment is unnecessary as you'll likely have everything you need at home. You need either a shower or a bathtub.

1. **Set the temperature of the shower or tub to as low as you can tolerate on the first day**: At first, any temperature that isn't your normal cozy shower will feel unpleasant. You'll want to jump out of the water immediately, but this is where you build mental strength. Remember, you are in control, not your body.
2. **Build up a tolerance to the cold and try to hit a set time**: If you're in the shower, try to stay in the cold water for 1 minute during your first week and then slowly work your way up to an ideal time of 5 minutes. The cold tub will be more challenging, as your entire body is constantly in the water. So, try to make it for the first 30 seconds and build up at a slower interval until you hit 5 minutes.
3. **Sessions per week**: The number of sessions you decide to use is entirely up to you. Personally, I have a cold shower every day as I find them very refreshing. And as for the cold tubs, they could be a good choice whenever you need that extra pep in your step.
4. **Making it more challenging**: Finally, once you master cold water exposure, you might ask how you can make this more difficult? When it comes to cold showers, we are limited in how cold we can make them as we can't lower the temperature anymore. We can increase the number of cold showers we have each week and increase the length of the cold shower. When it comes to the cold tubs, and you're feeling very confident, you can begin adding ice to your cold water. Be careful not to spill any ice on the bathroom floor, as they can be a real slip hazard (trust me on that one!). Adding ice will send your cold tubs to another level of pain, so take your time and build up slowly.

Remember that this therapy is not for everyone, so consult your doctor if you have any health issues. However, suppose it's suited for you. In that case, it can be a pleasant and effective approach to raise your mood and help you recover faster after exercise and live a longer, healthier life.

7

ACADEMIC SUCCESS

I joined school as quite a shy, average kid in each class. And as most kids do, I spent most of my early school years trying to make friends and fit in. Somewhere around my 16th birthday, I became more interested in my education. It probably had something to do with all my family relations asking me what I wanted to be when I got older. I wasn't sure how to answer that question, and I wasn't too worried as I had plenty of time to figure things out. Once I began focusing on school, I noticed certain classes I naturally excelled in. They were the classes that required a good memory, like geography, history, and science. These subjects came naturally to me, and I enjoyed them a lot. However, I couldn't say the same about the rest of my subjects, where I would often struggle to get good grades.

I soon decided on what I wanted to study in college. Since I absolutely loved science, I decided I wanted to pursue biochemistry as a career. This was a great choice as there were plenty of jobs in the pharmaceutical industry. One problem, though, was my current grades weren't good enough to qualify for this course.

At the beginning of my final year, I sat down and analyzed where I was. I was a C student in maths, French, and woodworking. If I wanted to reach my goal and head to college that year, I would need to improve each of those subjects along with others to have a chance. As you might have read in some of my other work, I became a scientist and have worked in the pharmaceutical industry for some of the biggest companies in the world. So, I made it through that final year in school. But how? Well, that's precisely what this chapter is about, what turned me into a top student. I'll be sharing all the learnings, tips, and tricks I picked up along the way that completely transformed my grades and made me a much better student.

HOW AN A+ STUDENT ACTS IN SCHOOL

Most of the information you need to learn in school or college is taught in class. The teacher oversees how fast the class goes, and you can't pause or slow them down like you can with reading or learning on your own. Although, if you watch a recorded class, you can pause and go back; it might not be as exciting as a live class. Using good strategies to pay attention in class and remember what you learned is essential. At first, it was challenging to implement these tips into my daily routine. Still, as I continued to practice, I noticed a significant improvement in my grades and overall academic performance. I always prioritized my studies, set achievable goals, and practiced active reading and note-taking. I also habitually sought help when I needed it, whether from my professors or classmates.

The most significant difference these tips made in my academic journey was that they helped me develop a growth mindset. Instead of feeling overwhelmed and defeated, I approached each challenge as an opportunity to learn and grow. And before I knew it, I went from being just an average student to graduating near the top of the class while being nominated for student of the year (I still have the plaque to prove it!).

I'm proud to say that these tips helped me do great in school and taught me valuable life skills that I carry with me to this day. I learned the importance of hàrd work, dedication, and perseverance and how these qualities can help me achieve Anything I set my mind to. Below are the tips that helped me, and they will also help set you up for academic success:

Before Class:

- The first thing I would do in the morning when I woke up was read over the material I knew the teacher would cover that day. Even if I didn't fully grasp the information, it meant that while the teacher explained the syllabus, it wasn't the first time I had seen it, which helped with comprehension.
- Review your notes from the last class to remember what you learned before the start of the next class:
- Write down any questions you have before class and listen for answers. If you need to, ask the teacher for clarification.

During Class

- Sit somewhere that helps you focus. For in-person classes, sit near the front. Find a quiet place without distractions for online courses and use headphones if needed.
- Don't use your phone or social media during class.
- Take good notes. Write down the main ideas and facts and use abbreviations to save time. If you need clarification, write it down to ask about it later. You won't have time to take full notes, so use shorthand and expand later at home.
- Stay focused on the class and pay attention to what the teacher says. If you lose focus, mark it in your notes.
- Listen carefully and look for important information like exam dates and homework assignments.

After Class

- Test yourself by asking and answering questions about the class/lecture.
- Summarize what you learned in your own words.
- Go over your notes again to make sure you understand everything.

Note: Being in class is a good time not only to be introduced to the course material but also to listen attentively to your teacher. See what subject, topics, and methods your teacher is coming back to time and time again. This gives you an early insight into what might be important to learn and what will likely feature in a test. Whether doing a lecture-based course at a college or taking classes at a high school, these strategies can help you stay focused, retain information, and maximize your educational experience.

In conclusion, the tips provided in this section are a great starting point if you want to improve your academic performance. Whether in high school or college, incorporating these strategies into your study habits can significantly impact your grades and overall success. By taking control of your education and adopting these tips, you can reach your full potential as a student. Let's take your study game to the next level and dive into creating effective notes in the next section. Get ready to learn how to turn your class lectures and textbook reading into memorable and efficient study materials!

CREATING NOTES

Creating great notes is a super important part of doing well in school. Think of it like creating a roadmap for your brain to follow. The better your notes, the easier it will be for you to remember what you learned and understand it when you need to use it later. In this section, we'll give tips to help you take notes that will set you up for success!

You can level up your learning by taking killer notes in class. By writing down what your teacher says, you can focus better and grasp the key ideas taught (UNC-Chapel Hill Learning Center, 2022). After class, your notes become your secret weapon for acing exams. Instead of feeling overwhelmed or having to rewatch whole lecture sections, you'll have a clear and organized guide to help you review. Trust me, having good notes will save you time, brainpower, and frustration when studying. Here's how to do it:

Jot down the important stuff: Write down key dates, facts, and examples your teacher mentions in class. If they write on the board, copy it down. If not, listen carefully and write down what's important.

Know your teacher's style: Some teachers write everything on the board, while others don't write Anything. With time, you'll learn what to listen for in each class.

Don't overdo it: Don't try to write down everything said in class. You'll miss the important parts. Focus on the key points and review the details after class if needed.

Ask for help: Be bold and ask your teacher to repeat something if you missed it. See your teacher afterward if you want to avoid asking in class.

Compare your notes: Keep your notes handy when you do your reading assignments, and compare what you wrote with what the readings say.

Study with a friend: Reviewing your notes with a friend can help reinforce what you're learning and alert you to errors.

Recopy your notes: Look over them when you get home and recopy them if needed. This will help you remember what you wrote (Note-Taking Tips (for Teens) - Nemours KidsHealth, n.d.).

Stay organized: Keep your notes for each subject in one place so you can find them easily when studying.

Methods of Taking Notes:

The best methods for taking notes are the mapping and boxing methods. We will explain each of them in detail. We will look at the best time to use these methods and their advantages.

Mapping Method

The mapping method is a way of taking notes that involves creating a visual representation of the information you are learning. This can be in the form of a diagram, chart, or mind map. This method aims to help you connect and understand the relationships between different ideas. It's best to use the mapping method when dealing with complex information with many interrelated parts, such as history, biology, or psychology. The visual representation helps you to see the big picture and makes it easier to remember the information.

One of the advantages of the mapping method is that it helps you to organize information in a way that makes sense to you. You can use colors, symbols, and images to help you remember important details. It's also a great way to spot connections and relationships between ideas you might have missed while taking traditional notes. Another advantage is that the mapping method allows for a more active learning experience. You are not just passively reading or listening to information but actively engaging with the material and making connections between ideas. This helps you to understand better and retain the information. Below is a simple way to practice the mapping method of note-taking:

1. Start by writing your notes' main topic or subject in the center of the page. For example, if you're taking notes on a lecture about ancient Egypt, write "Ancient Egypt" in the center of the page.
2. Next, draw branches out from the center, like the spokes of a wheel. These branches will represent the main subtopics or themes of your notes. For example, you might draw one branch for "Pharaohs," one for "Pyramids," and one for "Religion."

3. Under each subtopic branch, write down the key points or details you want to remember. For example, under the "Pharaohs" branch, you might write down the names of some important pharaohs and their accomplishments.
4. Use arrows, symbols, and other visual cues to connect related ideas and show how they relate. For example, use a star symbol to show an important point or draw arrows between related subtopics.
5. Don't worry too much about making everything look perfect or following a specific format. The mapping method is meant to be flexible and adaptable to your style of thinking and note-taking. Just focus on capturing the key ideas and connections in a way that makes sense to you.

Boxing Method

The boxing method of taking notes is a visual way of organizing information that makes it easier to understand and remember. In this method, you use a box to separate and organize ideas, facts, or information about a particular topic. To use the boxing method, draw a box around each key idea, concept, or fact and write it inside. You can also use different colors or symbols to differentiate between different types of information or highlight important points. One advantage of the boxing method is that it makes it easier to see the relationships between different pieces of information and how they all fit together. This can help you understand complex information more easily and remember it better. It also makes reviewing and studying your notes easier, as all the related information is organized in one place.

Another advantage of the boxing method is its highly visual approach to note-taking. It can be beneficial for students who learn better visually. It can also be a great option for students who struggle with keeping their notes organized, as it provides a clear structure for organizing information. The boxing method is a good choice for taking notes on any subject involving a lot of information, such as history, science, or literature.

It can also be useful for taking notes during meetings, lectures, or presentations. It helps you quickly and easily identify the most important points (The Best Note-Taking Methods for College Students & Serious Note-takers | GoodNotes Blog, n.d.). Below is a simple way to practice the boxing method of taking notes:

1. Start by drawing a square or rectangle on paper or in a note-taking app. This will be your "box" for taking notes.
2. In the top left corner of the box, write your notes' main topic or subject. For example, if you're taking notes on a lecture about literature, you might write "Literature" in the top left corner.
3. Divide the box into four quadrants by drawing one line down the center and one line across the middle. You should now have four smaller boxes within the larger box.
4. Label each quadrant with a subtopic or theme related to the main topic. For example, you might label the top right quadrant "Genres," the bottom left quadrant "Authors," and so on.
5. As you listen to the lecture or read the text, write down key points and details related to each subtopic in its respective quadrant. For example, in the "Genres" quadrant, you might write down different types of literature, such as poetry, drama, and fiction.
6. Use arrows, lines, and other visual cues to connect related ideas and show how they relate. For example, you might use an arrow to show how a particular author's work fits a certain genre.

Paper Notes and Electronic Notes

There are two ways to take notes: writing by hand or typing on a laptop or tablet device. The key to choosing between these two options is figuring out which will help you learn and remember information the best.

Handwritten notes are good because they can help you retain information better. Still, they can be slow if you're trying to take notes quickly during a fast-paced lecture. Digital notes, on the other hand, are fast and clean, but they can make it easy to get distracted by other things on your device. I found it helpful to first take quick notes on my laptop during class, and that night while going over my information from the day, I would make handwritten notes that I could use to study later. It's all about finding the method that works best for you!

(Communications, 2022)·

In conclusion, note creation is critical to effective learning and information retention. Whether you prefer mapping, boxing, handwritten notes, digital notes, or combining both, choosing the best method for you and your learning style is key.

STUDY TIPS

Okay, let's move on from note-taking but stay on the theme of study tips and tricks. In this section, I'll outline some techniques I found helpful during my studies. These tips will help you get more done quickly and maximize your potential. So, if you're looking for a quick and easy way to step up your study game, look no further. Get ready to hit the books with confidence with these tips!

Print vs. Electronics

Have you ever noticed that when you read from a screen, you don't seem to understand it as well as when reading from a piece of paper? Well, you're not alone! Studies have found that when people read on-screen, they often don't realize they're not retaining the information as well as when they read in print. According to psychologists and neuroscientists, our brain must work harder to understand text when we read on-screen because it has to use different networks of cells than it does when we read in print, and our brain adjusts accordingly.

So, when you're reading a school assignment on your phone, your brain might be in "skim mode" from scrolling through TikTok, but this mode might not be the best for understanding a classic book like

To Kill a Mockingbird. The faster you read on a screen, the less likely you will absorb all the ideas. So, next time you have a big reading assignment, try breaking away from the screen and picking up a good old piece of paper!

Active Recall

When trying to study and learn, there are better ways than just reading and rereading your notes. A lot of research shows that it's not very effective and doesn't help you remember things well. The best way to learn is through "active recall," which means testing yourself by creating questions from the information you're trying to learn and answering them. Follow the steps outlined below to learn how to practice active recall:

1. Start by selecting a topic you want to learn or review. It could be a subject in school or something you're interested in learning more about.
2. Read or study the material, taking notes as needed.
3. Close the book or put away your notes and try to recall as much information as possible about the topic.
4. Write down everything you can remember, even if you're unsure if it's accurate.
5. Check your notes or the textbook to see how much you got right, and make corrections to your recall notes as needed.
6. Repeat this process for several different topics or sections of your course material.
7. Test yourself periodically by trying to recall the information again, either by writing it down or explaining it out loud to someone else.
8. Use flashcards, quiz apps, or other study tools to help you practice active recall on the go or when you have free time.

Practice Tests

Testing yourself is a great way to learn. Instead of just reading a chapter or watching a video, try to see how much you can remember. This is called "practice testing." It's like taking a quiz to see how much you know. Doing this often, but with small quizzes, is a super effective way to learn.

Here are a few ways you can try practice testing:

- Take an online quiz after reading a class assignment.
- Take a quiz at the start of class.
- Take a quiz at the end of class.
- Try to answer a question from a previous class period.

Some tips to make practice testing work even better:

- Focus on the most important things you need to learn.
- Don't worry too much about getting a good grade.
- Try to answer short questions instead of just multiple choice.
- Get feedback on your answers. It will help you learn.
- Wait a little while before looking at the answers.
- Make sure you take practice quizzes throughout the semester.

Believe me; practice testing works! People sometimes think it's boring or not helpful, but studies show it's better than just reading the same thing repeatedly (A. Practice Testing - Teaching Improvement Guide, n.d.).

Leave the Phone in Another Room

Have you ever found yourself constantly staring at your phone even when you're supposed to be doing something important like studying or working? Well, it turns out that having your phone near you can make it harder for you to concentrate. Research shows that having your phone on the desk, even if turned off, can lower your ability to focus and process information (Why you should keep your phone in another room while Working or Studying, 2018). So, to be more productive or do well on a test, keep your phone in another room while working or studying.

This way, you won't be tempted to look at it and can focus all your attention on what you're doing. And who knows, you might even like it better without your phone around all the time!

Don't Focus on One Subject

Studying can be confusing and overwhelming, especially when you have many subjects to learn. Some people think it's better to focus on one subject a day, but studies show that it's better to study multiple subjects daily. This helps keep your brain from getting bored and burning out and enables you to remember the information better. Instead of focusing on one subject all day, try mixing things up and studying a little of everything each day. This gives your brain time to process the information, making you less likely to get confused between subjects. Another tip is to start with the subject you find the most difficult and do that first thing. You're at your sharpest when you begin studying, and you'll need all your brain power to tackle your toughest challenge. Then move on to your second most demanding subject and so on, leaving you with your favorite subject for last when you are beginning to burn out—making it easier to push through the mental lag.

Try to use any free time you have for studying, even if it's just 20 minutes between classes. This way, you'll be more prepared for your next class and won't forget the information you learned earlier. Remember, there's no right way to learn, so find what works for you (Should I Study One Subject a Day? - the Productive Engineer, 2021).

Use Tutors or Advisors

Tutoring is a way to get extra help with school. Instead of having a teacher who helps many students simultaneously, you'll get to work with a teacher or tutor who focuses on you (Benefits of Tutoring - How Does Tutoring Help Students? | Oxford Learning, 2017). This makes it easier for you to understand what you're learning. Tutoring can prepare you for tests and exams and make you feel more confident. You can also ask your tutor questions without feeling shy. Tutoring is a good choice if you're having trouble keeping up in school or want to do even better in certain subjects.

Active Reading

Reading is tough, especially in college. It can be a lot to handle, and you might feel like you can't stay focused, understand, or remember what you read. But don't worry, lots of students feel the same way. The good news is that you can make reading easier using simple strategies. Active reading is the key! When you actively engage with what you're reading, you remember it better than copying notes word for word or scanning the pages.

Before reading, you can do a few things to help you understand and remember what you read. First, figure out why you're reading the material and what you need to get out of it. Consider what you already know about the topic, and list things you want to learn while reading. Preview the text by looking at headings, pictures, and bold words. Break the reading into smaller chunks and take breaks in between to rest your brain. If you're reading from a screen, consider printing it out or taking breaks more often to avoid eye strain.

While reading, make sure you stay focused and engaged. Check-in with yourself to make sure you're not getting distracted. Try annotating the text by marking down key ideas and important information. Summarize what you read and ask critical thinking questions like "What differences exist between . . .?" or "What evidence can you present for . . .?" These tips will help you stay focused, understand, and remember what you read (UNC-Chapel Hill Learning Center, 2022).

In conclusion, effective studying involves a combination of various strategies and techniques that are tailored to everyone's learning style. It is important to find a balance between active and passive learning, as well as to incorporate regular breaks and exercise into your study routine. With all these tips in mind, it is possible to maximize your retention and recall of information.

Now, let's look at some scientifically proven study methods.

SCIENTIFICALLY PROVEN STUDY METHODS

This section will discuss scientifically proven study methods developed by psychologists. These methods have been tested and proven effective in helping students retain information and perform better on exams. These approaches are a great starting point to improve your study habits and boost your academic performance. So, let's dive in and discover how we can turn ourselves into super students!

The Curve of Forgetting

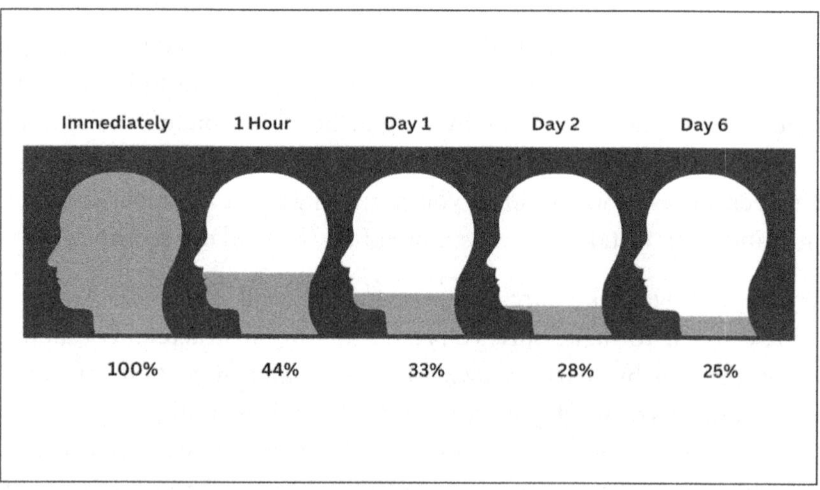

Imagine you just learned a new song on the guitar, and you're super excited to show it off to your friends. But the next day, when you try to play it, you realize you can't quite remember all the chords and strumming patterns. This is what's known as the "Curve of Forgetting." The curve was discovered by a German psychologist named Hermann Ebbinghaus in the late 1800s. He found that our memories of new information fade over time unless we actively work to remember them (What Is the Forgetting curve? 2022). In other words, if you don't practice that new song, you'll gradually forget how to play it.

Think of the Ebbinghaus curve as a graph that shows how much of what you learned yesterday you'll remember today and how much you'll remember a week from now. The graph starts high, meaning you can recall it well right after you learn something. But then it dips down, which means that over time, you'll forget more and more of what you learned (Classics in the History of Psychology -- Ebbinghaus (1885/1913) Chapter 1, n.d.).

The good news is that the Ebbinghaus curve isn't a line that heads straight downward. It starts to level off, which means that at some point, you'll stop forgetting so quickly. And if you actively review and practice what you've learned, you can keep that information in your memory for longer. You can use the Ebbinghaus curve of forgetting to study better by understanding how your memory works. According to the curve, you tend to forget most of the information you learn within the first 24 hours. If you only study once, you will likely forget most of the information when you need to use it. However, returning to the same material within the same 24-hour period dramatically increases your chances of remembering. In addition, the curve also suggests that the more you repeat the information, the more it becomes consolidated in your long-term memory. So, the more you study, the better you will remember the information in the long run.

Thus, to make the most of the Ebbinghaus curve of forgetting, study in spaced intervals and review the information regularly. This will help you remember the information better and perform better in exams!

Leitner System

Flashcards are a popular tool to help you remember things while studying. The idea is that repetition helps you learn, but just using flashcards repeatedly might not be enough if you're trying to learn something complicated. A guy named Sebastian Leitner came up with a way to use flashcards that's even better, called the Leitner System. It's based on the idea of spaced repetition, which means spreading out your studying over time instead of trying to learn everything all at once (The Leitner System: How Does it Work? 2021).

To start with the Leitner System, you need to make flashcards (one for each idea you want to learn), put them into boxes, and mark when you want to study each box on your calendar. Here's how it works: you start with all your flashcards in Box 1 and study them daily. If you get a flashcard right, move it to Box 2 and study it every other day. If you get it wrong, you move it back to Box 1. Repeat this until all your flashcards are in Box 3, which you study once a week.

The Leitner System is better than just using flashcards because it gets your brain working more. The Leitner System helps you keep the information in your memory longer by answering questions and trying to remember what you learned. When we try to learn a lot of information simultaneously, our brains can't keep up, and we forget most of it. But with spaced repetition and active recall, our brain has time to process what we're learning and remember it better (The Leitner System for flashcards: how to elevate your memory and learning, 2022). Even if you're used to a different way of studying, the Leitner System still has the basic idea of using flashcards, making it even more effective. Whether studying for a test, learning a new language, or trying to pick up a new hobby, the Leitner System can help you reach your learning objectives.

The Feynman Technique

The Feynman Technique is a learning method that can help you study smarter, not harder. This technique was named after Nobel Prize-winning physicist Richard Feynman, who used it to help him understand complex scientific concepts. Here's how the Feynman Technique works: when trying to understand a new concept or information, try to explain it in your own words as if you were teaching it to someone else. This helps you identify gaps in your knowledge and understand the material more deeply (The Feynman Technique: The Best Way to Learn Anything, 2021).

You can use the Feynman Technique in the following way:

1. Write down the concept or information you're trying to understand.
2. Explain the concept or information in your own words, as if you were teaching it to a friend or younger sibling. Use simple language and avoid technical terms as much as possible.
3. Identify areas where your explanation is unclear or you struggle to understand the material. These are the areas you need to focus on.
4. Go back to your textbook or other resources and fill in any gaps in your knowledge.
5. Repeat the process of explaining the concept in your own words until you feel confident that you fully understand it.

The Feynman Technique works because it forces you to actively engage with the material and think critically instead of passively reading it. When you explain a concept in your own words, you must understand it at a deeper level than just memorizing definitions or facts. This leads to a better understanding of the material, which will help you perform better on exams and tests. So, you can use the Feynman Technique to study for better grades by breaking down complex subjects into simple explanations and filling in any gaps in your understanding. With practice, you'll find that you can learn and remember information more easily, and you'll feel more confident and prepared for your exams.

In conclusion, scientifically proven study methods such as the Ebbinghaus curve of forgetting, the Leitner System, and the Feynman Technique are effective ways to improve your studying habits and retain information better. Experts in the field of psychology have developed these methods. They have been proven to be successful in improving memory retention and overall learning abilities. Incorporating these techniques into your study routine allows you to maximize your study time and achieve better grades. In the next section, I'll share my "secret" study tips I have found to be very beneficial over the years. I don't see many others using these simple tricks, so if you begin using them, you'll have a huge advantage over the competition, so take note.

Secret Study Tips That Few Others Practice

Welcome to the final section, where you will discover the secret study tips few people know and practice. These tips have been proven to enhance the learning experience and help students achieve their full potential. These tips are not widely known or practiced but have been kept secret and passed down from successful students to their peers. This section will teach you new and innovative ways to study and improve your grades. Get ready to uncover the hidden gems of studying and transform how you approach learning!

Know What Your Teacher or Lecturer Is Asking Before You Begin Writing

Have you ever had a teacher get mad because you didn't properly answer the question they asked in an assignment or exam? Well, that's a common problem that a lot of students face. But don't worry because we have a secret technique that can help you make sure you answer the question the right way! It's called the Question Analysis technique. Here's how it works:

1. Read the question twice to ensure you understand what it asks.
2. Look for "topic words"—these words tell you the question. But watch out because sometimes the question might only want you to write about one part of that topic.
3. Look for "restricting words"—words or phrases that narrow the topic and make it more specific. This is what your teacher really wants you to write about.
4. Look for "instruction words" that tell you what to do. For example, suppose your teacher wants you to describe something. In that case, your answer will be different than if they want you to assess something critically.
5. Finally, rewrite the question in your own words to ensure you understand it correctly. But ensure you stay close to the original question, so you don't change the meaning (Question Analysis, n.d.).

Using the above five steps, you'll be able to ensure you answer the question correctly and get the best grade possible!

Alpha Waves

Have you tried studying something hard but couldn't remember what you read? Well, there's music that can help with that! It's not just any music, though. It's special music called alpha waves. Alpha waves are signals in your brain that help you relax, be more creative, and remember things better. It's like they turn on a switch in your brain that enables you to focus better. Scientists think alpha waves come from a part of your brain called the thalamus, which helps you sleep better and be more alert during the day.

By listening to alpha wave music, you can boost your brain power, absorb new knowledge more easily, and be more creative. This will help you pass your tests and exams with ease. Alpha brain waves music can be found on various platforms such as YouTube, Spotify, Apple Music, and other streaming services. Search for "alpha waves music" or "alpha brain waves music," and you will find various options. Trust me, give the alpha waves a try the next time you need to study material or when you're reading something you have to comprehend. You'll notice a laser focus you haven't felt before.

Changing Your Study Setting

New research shows that changing your study environment can help you remember what you learned better! For example, the idea that everyone has a "learning style" (visual, auditory, etc.) and should have a designated study area is false.

Studies have shown that varying your study environment can improve your memory. In a classic experiment from 1978, psychologists found that college students who studied a list of 40 vocabulary words in two different rooms (one without windows and messy, the other modern and with a view) did much better on a test than students who studied the words twice, in the same room. More recent studies have confirmed these results for different subjects.

This is because the brain connects what it's learning and its surroundings, whether you're aware of it or not (Change Up Your Study Spaces for Better Recall, 2013). So, if you're a college student who's always on the move or loves to work in different coffee shops, don't feel bad about changing things up. You're helping your memory! And for the rest of us who sometimes feel stuck at our desks, taking breaks and changing our environment can also be a great way to improve our memory.

Sleep

Staying up late to study or work is something a lot of people do even when they're feeling stressed out. But sleeping is important because it helps your brain remember things you learned during the day. If you don't sleep well, you'll have difficulty remembering what you studied. Your brain works best when you're asleep, and different stages of sleep help with different types of learning. For example, dreaming helps with creative problem-solving and enables you to remember information you learned that day. Not getting enough sleep also affects your mood and mental health, making you irritable and angry, which won't help with learning.

Many teenagers don't get enough sleep, and it can lead to lower grades. It's important to ensure you get enough sleep so your brain can do its job and help you learn better (Active Health, n.d.).

In conclusion, incorporating these secret study tips, such as understanding what your lecturer is asking before beginning to write, utilizing alpha waves, changing your study setting, and prioritizing sleep, can greatly enhance your studying effectiveness. These unique approaches to studying can improve your understanding of the material and make the studying experience more enjoyable and fulfilling. By taking a personalized and innovative approach to your studies, you can reach your full potential and achieve academic success. So why not try these secret study tips and see their positive impact on your grades and overall learning experience!

REVIEW

Before you read the conclusion to this book, I would like to share a personal message with you all; Writing this book has brought my life immeasurable happiness; I genuinely hope reading it brings your life the same joy. For over a decade, I have been obsessing with self-improvement and developing my skills to one day call myself a success. I'm still on my journey to success and happiness, and that's okay because life is most enjoyable when you are striving to improve and chasing goals. A man needs a mountain to climb to feel challenged and feel he is accomplishing something. I suggest you use the teachings in this book, find something you are passionate about, and never stop trying to improve until you reach your goal. One day, you'll wake up, and when you look in the mirror, you'll see a man standing before you that you and your family can be proud of.

If I could ask one favor from you, the reader, it is to help me spread my message of teenage self-improvement and build a community of like-minded people, all trying to develop as a person. Please consider leaving a review of this book on Amazon. Reviews are the lifeblood of our business, and it helps us get this book into the hands of more people who need it. If you can leave a review, please do. And if not, please ask your parent or whoever purchased the book to leave a review on Amazon.

Please scan the QR code below, and you will be redirected to our review page on Amazon; I will read every single review personally.

If you ever need to contact me with any questions on this book, please feel free to reach out to me at the email below:

admin@teenlifeskill.com

CONCLUSION

Now that we have concluded our book, I want to reemphasize the immense importance of the information contained within. If you are a young guy, like the one I was as a teen, you're not satisfied with mediocrity and want to get the most out of your life. We don't all start at the same point or life position. Some people reading this book might be upper to middle class and have a great life, or perhaps a person reading this book might be struggling now and not have much money or support. No matter your situation, we all need the teachings in this book just the same.

Life can sometimes seem overwhelming as young gentlemen, and we can become lost. This feeling of being lost can continue into adulthood and remain if we don't address the problems. Too many young men today never learn how to become a man, and they waste their teenage years playing video games and eating candy. This is what's called instant gratification, meaning we want pleasure in the here and now. But suppose you are willing to sacrifice pleasure at the moment and delay that gratification. In that case, that's where the real growth happens.

Let's take a quick look at an example of this . . .

A Life of Instant Gratification

You wake up around noon after having snoozed your alarm clock five times. You head downstairs and see a box of sugary cereal or a bowl of fruit with some eggs on the table. You choose the cereal. Now it's time to decide what to do with your day. Your friends message you and ask if you want to come to the game with them as they need another starter, but you decide to stay home and play video games instead as you "can't be bothered to go play sports." As the day passes, you remember you have an exam next week, and you say okay, I'll study after just one more game. One game lead to another, and you never study. Fast forward, you take the test, get the results, and fail.

A Life of Delayed Gratification

You wake up to the sound of the alarm you had set the night before. You turn off the alarm and immediately jump out of bed, brush your teeth, and wash your face. You head downstairs and see two options for breakfast, some sugary cereal or some fruit and eggs. You take the fruit and eggs. Suddenly you get a phone call. It's your friend offering you a ride to the game as they need another starter as someone has been injured since the last game. You jump at the opportunity as it is great exercise and a chance to socialize with your friends. You arrive home after the game and just remember you have a test next week. You really wanted to play video games for a while before bed, so you have another choice. You decide to play video games next weekend and sit down to study. Fast forward, you take the test and get an A+.

So, what's the difference between the two stories? In one story, the person constantly looks for immediate pleasure or gratification, leading him to repeatedly make poor decisions that will negatively affect his life. The person willing to delay the gratification for another time had a much more productive and healthy day. By delaying the urge to sleep in, he has more hours in the day, and by choosing a healthy breakfast, he increases his chances of having a body he is proud of.

By engaging with his friends and playing the sports game, he feels a sense of accomplishment after the game and ensures he maintains his friendships for the future. Finally, he gets a fantastic grade on his test by delaying the pleasure of playing video games. So, the story's moral here is that we make hundreds of decisions daily. Sleep in, yes, or no? Eat a healthy breakfast, yes, or no? Play video games, yes, or no? To grow up to be successful, wealthy, and happy, you must constantly try to make the next right decision. If you do this for long enough, I guarantee you will reach the desired level of success you want in life.

Being a man is not easy, but for you to feel happy and satisfied in life, you must become the best version of a man you can be. Today men's mental health is at an all-time low. I believe it is because too many of us have turned away from classical male values and roles. Suppose we return to a more masculine way of living. In that case, this will satisfy that natural urge within us that can cause anxiety and depression if we ignore it. A man should take on responsibility in his life. He is responsible for looking after the people who are closest to him. He should support his father, mother, brothers, sisters, and other relations and friends. Be a protector, try to provide for the people you love, and don't be afraid to stand up and speak up for what's right. Don't put substances in your body that will hurt you, such as alcohol, too much sugar, or fast food. Remember, your body is your temple to take care of yourself.

Harness the power of your mind and choose the values you think are the most important to you by using the lessons in Chapter 1 and Chapter 2. Build upon your social skills to make more friends, impress during job interviews and when the time comes, speak to girls. Learn how to speak and communicate confidently, as shown in Chapter 3, as this is one of life's most important skills.

When the time comes, and you're ready to begin dating, then take the advice in this book and go out and find your partner. The key here is to be very respectful, no matter the outcome of speaking to someone you like. Be confident also, and don't fear rejection. The fact that you were willing to try speaking to a girl shows real confidence.

Use all the skills and advice in Chapter 5 to ensure you're smelling and looking your best for all life's situations. Then make sure to employ all the learnings in Chapter 6 to take the best care of your body and mind. Remember, our bodies are like a house we must own and live in for the next 70–80 years, so take the best possible care of it. Limit junk food, sleep over 7.5 hours every night and exercise intensely 3–4 times a week. Not only will this keep you healthy, but you'll look your absolute best also.

The last chapter is about studying effectively, but why is studying essential to becoming a man? The truth is that today's world is very competitive when it comes to finding a job or trying to get into college. Everyone is battling for the same position, and to be successful, you need to ensure you're a step above the competition. Use the study techniques included in this book and become the best student you can be. Never stop learning, as this is when you stagnate and stop growing. Whether you are a plumber, doctor, mechanic, or dentist, never stop learning and trying to improve your skills, as constant growth is an important part of life.

Finally, the key takeaway from this book is that success in all areas of life may be attained through the development of constructive habits, self-awareness, and continual learning and improvement. Using the principles discussed in this book, you can establish a growth mindset, improve social skills, form meaningful relationships, and achieve academic success. So, now that you have all the tools put them to use! Success is a journey, not a destination. Therefore, take little steps toward your goals every day. Don't be afraid to seek assistance or support along the journey. Remember that the most important thing is to believe in yourself and never give up on your aspirations.

DISCLAIMER

The Publisher has made every effort to ensure the information contained within this book was correct at the time of publishing. Our company Teen Life Skills, is dedicated to providing accurate information to our readers regarding the subject matter discussed in this book. The Publisher, the author, and the company Teen Life Skills assume no responsibility for errors, inaccuracies, omissions, or any inconsistencies herein and hereby disclaim any liability to any party for loss, damage, or disruption caused by errors or omissions.

The publication is designed to provide valuable information for our readers. However, this information is not supposed to substitute direct expert assistance. If such assistance is required, the services of an expert should be sought.

Teen Life Skills advise you the reader to take full responsibility for your own safety and understand your own constraints before reading this book. Prior too practicing the skills described within, please understand the techniques fully and any risks that may lay within your own capabilities to perform, practice or demonstrate the skills.

BIBLIOGRAPHY

PLEASE SCAN THE QR CODE BELOW TO ACCESS THIS BOOK BIBLIOGRAPHY

Made in United States
Orlando, FL
25 August 2023

36427384R00068